IAN T. RAMSEY

Makers of the Modern Theological Mind

Bob E. Patterson, Editor

KARL BARTH by *David L. Mueller*
DIETRICH BONHOEFFER by *Dallas M. Roark*
RUDOLF BULTMANN by *Morris Ashcraft*
CHARLES HARTSHORNE by *Alan Gragg*
WOLFHART PANNENBERG by *Don Olive*
TEILHARD DE CHARDIN by *Doran McCarty*
EMIL BRUNNER by *J. Edward Humphrey*
MARTIN BUBER by *Stephen M. Panko*
SÖREN KIERKEGAARD by *Elmer H. Duncan*
REINHOLD NIEBUHR by *Bob E. Patterson*
H. RICHARD NIEBUHR by *Lonnie D. Kliever*
GERHARD VON RAD by *James L. Crenshaw*
ANDERS NYGREN by *Thor Hall*
FRIEDRICH SCHLEIERMACHER by *C. W. Christian*
HANS KÜNG by *John Kiwiet*
IAN T. RAMSEY by *William B. Williamson*
CARL F. H. HENRY by *Bob E. Patterson*

Makers of the Modern Theological Mind

Bob E. Patterson, Editor

IAN T. RAMSEY

by William B. Williamson

Word Books, Publisher, Waco, Texas
A Division of Word, Inc.

Ian T. Ramsey

Copyright © 1982 by Word, Incorporated. All rights reserved. No portion
of this book may be reproduced in any form without the written permission
of the publisher, except for brief excerpts in magazine reviews.

Library of Congress Cataloging in Publication Data

Williamson, William Bedford, 1918–
 Ian T. Ramsey.

 (Makers of the modern theological mind; v. 15)
 Bibliography: p.
 1. Ramsey, Ian T. 2. Philosophical theology—History
of doctrines—20th century. 3. Empirical theology—History
of doctrines—20th century. 4. Christianity and
language—History of doctrines—20th century. I. Ramsey,
Ian T. I. Title. II. Series.
BX5199.R22W54 1982   201   82–15876
ISBN 0–8499–2947–4

Printed in the United States of America

In memory of
two magnificient bishops
of the church

FRANK WILLIAM STERRETT

Sometime Bishop of Bethlehem

and

IAN THOMAS RAMSEY

Sometime Bishop of Durham

Shepherds, Friends and Exemplars

Contents

Editor's Preface

Who are the thinkers that have shaped Christian theology in our time? This series tries to answer that question by providing a reliable guide to the ideas of the men who have significantly charted the theological seas of our century. In the current revival of theology, these books will give a new generation the opportunity to be exposed to significant minds. They are not meant, however, to be a substitute for a careful study of the original works of these makers of the modern theological mind.

This series is not for the lazy. Each major theologian is examined carefully and critically—his life, his theological method, his most germinal ideas, his weaknesses as a thinker, his place in the theological spectrum, and his chief contribution to the climate of theology today. The books are written with the assumption that laymen will read them and enter into the theological dialogue that is so necessary to the church as a whole. At the same time they are carefully enough designed to give assurance to a Ph.D. student in theology preparing for his preliminary exams.

Each author in the series is a professional scholar and theologian in his own right. All are specialists on, and in some cases have studied with, the theologians about whom they write. Welcome to the series.

BOB E. PATTERSON, Editor
Baylor University

Preface

The writing of this book has been a labor of love. The desire to give Ian Ramsey his due recognition as a pacesetting philosophical theologian and to assist in the explication of his contributions has been present in my mind and heart since the year of his untimely death, 1972. The book should have been written sooner, but events and circumstances caused some delay. Nevertheless, this work is offered as a tribute to the life, teachings and ministry of a man whom to know was to love. Indeed, I can rightly say that in my special experiences with Ramsey, both friendship and work with him changed my life and vocation; and for this I will be eternally grateful. From Ramsey I learned not only to fully appreciate the necessary grounding of all claims to knowledge in the empirical, but also to fully appreciate the areas of human knowledge which are empirical and "more." But most of all I learned from him the supreme importance of the human equation in learning, the primacy of a student's understanding and informed decision, and the inestimable value of an instructor's caring but relentless efforts to develop an intelligent and rational decision-making process.

How unfortunate for us that death cut short the potential influence of this remarkable teacher and churchman. It is my hope that this book will provide some vicarious good will and appreciation of Ramsey and his unique and helpful contributions and person.

The writing of this book has been a labor shared by many others. I am indebted to three friends who agreed to be readers of the manuscript in various stages of its development: Professor E. Russell Naughton of LaSalle College; Professor George G. Storey, my colleague at Ursinus College; and Professor Thomas J. Young of Gwynedd-Mercy College. These scholars were careful editors who pointed out my errors and ambiguities and Professor Young actually assisted me in several areas of rewriting, most specifically the paraphrasing of a number of quotations. I am thankful for the enlightened services of my typist, Carol Lucas Custer, a former honors student of mine at Ursinus, who provided insights and good humor to an otherwise mechanical procedure. Thanks also are due to the Reference staff of the Myrin Library of Ursinus College, as well as to several individuals who were helpful, namely, Doris H. Fozard, Virginia M. Daly, and those with whom I live and work. Finally, I am grateful for the interest, enthusiasm and encouragement of Bob E. Patterson, editor of this book and series, "Makers of the Modern Theological Mind." He is a caring and understanding person and a true professional.

IAN T. RAMSEY

I. Ian Thomas Ramsey:
Philosopher, Theologian and Churchman
A Biographical Survey

1. *Introduction*

At the time of my first meeting with Ian Ramsey, he was billed as the Rev. Canon and Professor Ian Thomas Ramsey, Nolloth Professor of the Philosophy of the Christian Religion in the University of Oxford—the Bohlen Lecturer of the Philadelphia Divinity School of the Episcopal Church. The subject of his series of three lectures was concerned with the empirical placing of religious discourse. I made arrangements to attend all three lectures and determined to try to talk with him personally. Convinced that Ramsey was truly one of the more important philosophical theologians of the contemporary theological scene, I felt he was one of the principal architects of an empirically oriented Christian theology. My reading of his works, at that time limited to *Religious Language* and several articles, had impressed me with his efforts to clarify the language of theology by applying to it the tools of analytic philosophy. I was not disappointed.

Ramsey was a giant of a man—but not in stature, it is

true. Still he manifested a true greatness in erudition, self-confidence, poise and good will. He was a philosopher who radiated the best enlightenment of both the classical mode of matching every problem with a "key" and the contemporary mode of language analysis. His consistency and command of explication and illumination of thesis and supporting evidence and argument were compelling and magnetic. Even on our first meeting, Ramsey revealed an encyclopedic grasp of both philosophy and theology and an awe-inspiring ability to reach into the Bible, social science, mathematics and science to illustrate his points of view and arguments. He lectured with extreme self-confidence and with an obvious determination to convince which, on rare occasions, was guilty of overkill. His seminars and conferences were conducted with similar verve and assurance. Further, in both lecture hall and in smaller sessions, Ramsey's consummate poise made it possible, yes, even easy for him to prompt discussion and criticism of his own position. But the most obvious of his characterisitics was his warm good will. Someone has said he had the disarming charm of a Santa Claus with a merry twinkle in his eye and the sly wit of a Scottish comedian. Regardless, those who knew him well and called him friend are unanimous in praising his caring personality and the constant good will he exuded.

2. Birth and Early Education

Ian Thomas Ramsey was born on 31 January 1915, in Kearsley, Bolton in a modest red-brick house so typical of urban Britain. The town itself is hardly outstanding, and except for its small industries of mining, a battery works and a tile factory would hardly merit any special attention. But it was Ramsey's birthplace and it must have influenced his early life.

He was the only child of Arthur and Mary Ramsey. Arthur was a British civil servant who was a post office employee in Bolton and finally became Postmaster of Norwich. Mary was from a Lancashire mining family, a woman small of stature but with the dynamic energy which gave vitality to the Ramsey family. It was Mary's stature and her drive which Ian inherited along with his father's gentleness and his painstaking thoroughness. Further, the Ramsey home provided a pervading influence of the Christian religion complete with family prayers, Bible reading and stories. And Ian always remained faithful to the values of his heritage. Indeed, his never-flagging interest in morality, related to and inspired by religion, had its roots in his Christian family. Another strong influence in Ramsey's religious thought was Ian's remembrance of his humble economic environment and especially of the depression, unemployment and poverty of the Lancashire area. No doubt this memory influenced his constant identification with and concern for the worker and those economically deprived and in need of a champion.

Ian's early schooling was begun in the primary school of St. John's Church (Anglican) in Farnworth near Bolton. From there he enrolled, at the age of ten, as a scholarship winner at Farnworth Grammar School, where he concentrated on Latin and soon was the outstanding student in his form. However, as his mind developed, he discovered abilities in mathematics, physics and chemistry. He earned "distinctions" in most of his subjects and held an office in the school's scientific society. Ian himself admitted that he was unsuccessful in athletics and sports, but confessed that he did enjoy cycling. Fortunately, Farnworth provided a good education and Ian had taken full advantage of it.

3. A Cambridge Undergraduate

On the basis of his grammar school accomplishments, he won both a scholarship at Manchester University and a place at Christ's College, Cambridge—a notable victory for a poor boy from Farnworth. Fortuitously, he also won a State Scholarship as well as one from the Lancashire County Council and he was able to matriculate at Cambridge. Ian's announced goal was to study mathematics and physics, or else perhaps study for civil service.

Cambridge represented many changes in Ian's life style. For one thing, his rather serious involvement in the life of the church, which he had established at home, seemed to vanish as he invested all of his time and interest in his studies. His early religious experiences in Sunday school, his confirmation and his friendship with the Vicar of St. John's had no carryover at Cambridge, and he kept mostly to himself, quite aware of his physical stature and his thick Lancashire accent. But mostly he felt the pinch of his tight economic condition. He lived in separated and drafty quarters and conscious of his budget (approximately 150 pounds a year), failed to eat properly and to take care of himself. His Spartan existence and personal neglect caused a cold to develop first into bronchitis and finally into tuberculosis. Thus in 1934, at the age of nineteen, he went to Papworth Sanitarium.

This hospitalization and subsequent convalescence brought about a change in Ian. He developed an interest in philosophy and theology and rekindled his basic love for the church. Some of this change came from his reading, but most of it was based on a helpful fellowship with the Rev. H. F. Woolnough, the Chaplain of Christ's College, as well as a number of divinity students who visited him. Such Christian fellowship brought out the natural warmth of young Ian and he responded by accepting the loving ministry they represented. But most of all he recognized that he had been given back his life by a loving God and believed that he had experienced a "spiritual awakening" which he would later describe in more philosophical language as a "disclosure."

Ian resumed his studies in October, 1935, with some restrictions on his activities—for instance, an early bedtime each day. Still, he achieved many honors: First Classes in Mathematical Tripos Part I, 1936; Moral Sciences Tripos Part II, 1938; Theological Tripos Part II (with distinction), 1939; Burney

Prizeman, 1938; Burney Student, 1939. Finally he won his M. A. in 1940. More important, perhaps, was the fact that Ian came under the influence of the Rev. Dr. Charles Raven, the Regius Professor of Divinity and the Master of the Rideout Society of which Ramsey was a member. It was Raven, concerned that religion and science should be blended, who guided Ian to develop a mature religious expression and transferred his hopes for the merger of philosophy and religion to his pupil. Another Cambridge influence was Ian's supervisor in philosophy, Professor A. C. Ewing, whose metaphysical interests influenced Ramsey's Burney Prize Essay in 1938. Indeed, Ewing's influence also was to become a lasting one, expressed in what Ramsey called an empirically "chastened" form.

4. Theological Education at Oxford

Following his successes at Cambridge, Ramsey turned to Oxford and enrolled at Ripon Hall, the Church of England Theological College, to prepare for ordination. It was at Ripon that Ian more fully developed his personality, for here he was recognized not only because of his intellectual abilities, but also because of his friendly and outgoing attitudes and behavior. He was regarded with affection and nicknamed "Panda," indicating he was one of the boys. Interestingly enough his first sermon was entitled, "Why be religious—isn't it enough to be good?" Obviously this was a question which needed his attention and one which he would answer in his own life by evidencing "both . . . and" rather than "either . . . or." This same drive for synthesis is also seen in his announced ambition to build a bridge between theology and philosophy.

Also, Professor C. H. Dodd has said that Ramsey had indicated to him that he had come to Oxford because of the antimetaphysical and antireligious philosophy so prevalent there. Ramsey announced that it was his hope to develop a new apologetic for religious propositions, and thus for Christian theology using the tools of logic and the methodology of philosophical analysis. Further, he revealed to a friend that it was his goal to return to Christ's College someday to accomplish his bridge building and apologetic constructing.

While at Ripon preparing for ordination, Ramsey was named Assistant Curate of the Anglican Parish of Headington Quarry, a village quite close to Oxford. There he served under the Rev. T. E. Beliben and lived with the Belibens in their Vicarage. With his usual enthusiasm and native drive, he entered unreservedly into the life of the parish. With particular responsibility for the youth of the parish, Ramsey assumed the leadership of the St. Christopher's Guild, which provided teachers for the Sunday school. The subject of Christian education was of such importance to him that he made improvement of the Sunday school the title of his ordination essay presented to the Bishop of Oxford, Dr. Kenneth Kirk. Needless to say, he advocated higher standards in both curriculum materials and in the quality of instruction.

It was in the parish of Haddington Quarry that he met and fell in love with Margretta (Margaret) McKay; the proposal of marriage which shortly followed, Ramsey called the "best decision I ever made." And he was quite right. Margretta provided for Ramsey an affectionate, calm and stable personal and family life that was good for him as a person, since he gave himself so fully and completely to others and to the ultimate goals of knowledge and the Christian religion. His interest in and concern for those he was instructing, counseling or just talking with was so intense that without Margretta's stability, the continuity she provided within and to his family, his self-giving to others might have strained his marriage and harmed his family. Those who came to know her because of Ian are convinced that he was right in saying that his choice of Margretta McKay Ramsey was in fact the best decision he ever made. She is a lovely person, a shy but witty individual and a gracious lady. And it was Margretta whose competent care and genuine Christian love made Ramsey's home, as the

Book of Common Prayer suggests, "a haven of blessing and of peace."

5. *Chaplain of Christ's College, Cambridge*

Ramsey returned to Christ's College, Cambridge as Chaplain in 1943 and was elected a Fellow and Director of Studies in Theology and Moral Science in 1944. The same year he was named University Lecturer in Divinity and Canon Theologian of Leicester Cathedral; and he was known as Canon Ramsey until he was named Bishop in 1966. His chaplaincy at Christ's College was not an easy post for Ramsey. In the first place it was wartime and he was a pacifist, and the more patriotic dons were persistent in their criticism of him. However, Ramsey accepted an appointment in the civilian defense as the college air raid and fire warden and gave himself to these duties as was his custom—with efficiency and vigor. Still he was always suspect among his more "patriotic" colleagues. Ramsey was not the preacher his predecessor Canon Raven was; nevertheless, he won the hearts of the students by the combination of his giant intellect and warm personality, as evidenced by his numerous and often amusing illustrations. In all he was a successful Chaplain not only because he was always available and sympathetically concerned, but also because he was interested in a wide variety of activities and societies from debating to table tennis.

His impact on Cambridge as a member of the University was as great as he had enjoyed as a student. As a lecturer he was a pioneer in the distribution of duplicated notes on his lectures and the name of Ramsey came to be associated with his well-known and appreciated effort to impart clarity along with content. His honors were many: Select Preacher and Hulsean Preacher, 1944, 1949, 1950 and 1956; Stanton Lecturer in Philosophy of Religion, 1947–1950. The notes from these latter lectures reveal a developing philosophical theology which accepted the injunctions of G. E. Moore and

Ludwig Wittgenstein. It was the aim of Ramsey's lectures to advance in a clear and rigorous manner the metaphysical doctrines of Berkeley toward a "new" metaphysics reconciled with empiricism.[2]

6. Nolloth Professor of the Philosophy of the Christian Religion, Oxford

On the retirement of Professor L. W. Grensted, Ramsey was invited to be a candidate for the chair of Nolloth Professor of the Philosophy of the Christian Religion in the University of Oxford in 1950. And as tempting as the invitation was, he joined with other philosophers in objecting to the stipulation that only Anglican communicants could be holders of the chair. Finally, after the chair's limitation was removed, Ramsey accepted election in 1951.

In many ways his election fulfilled his most cherished academic desire, to be at Oxford and to mount a challenge to logical positivism by using philosophical analysis to construct a new and convincing apologetic for the Christian religion. But what he found at Oxford among his colleagues in divinity was a conservative climate much more favorable to theology than to philosophy. Indeed, few chose to write in the philosophy of religion. He found a climate influenced by the more traditional apologetic of C. S. Lewis and a society of Christian dons who called themselves "The Metaphysicals" led by Austin Farrer, who was quite openly suspicious of the orthodoxy of Ramsey. Indeed, when Basil Mitchell put together a collection of essays by members of the metaphysicals entitled *Faith and Logic*,[3] Ramsey, the Nolloth Professor, was not invited to submit a paper.

However, the writings and criticisms of Wittgenstein were beginning to impress British thought, which was already reeling from the onslaught of A. J. Ayer's *Language, Truth and Logic*, published just before World War II. Ayer's book attracted the attention of almost everyone, including scholars. After the war Gilbert Ryle's *Concept of Mind* appeared in 1949. It was followed by the work of Stuart Hampshire, J. L. Austin, P. F. Strawson and R. M. Hare which opened a new chapter in the story of British philosophy. Fortunately, Ramsey understood the import of their work and reveled in sessions with them with much mutual profit. For instance, Hare acknowledged to me in a personal interview his regard for Ramsey and evidenced his regard by honoring Ramsey's request that he take part in Anglican discussion groups.

Ramsey's inaugural lecture given on 7 December 1951 was titled "Miracles: An Exercise in Logical Mapwork."[4] It represented both a personal statement of faith and a firm statement of his hope to establish a "descriptive" metaphysics in contrast to its usual "speculative" nature. It was in this lecture that he set forth his belief in personal existence, the "I" as "something more" than the empiricists allow. David Edwards reports that "Professor Ryle had been heard to express a courteous skepticism." Interestingly enough, Ramsey later took on Ryle on the subject of the "I," or "self-awareness," insisting on some area of the self which is "observationally elusive," or as his title suggested, "The Systematic Elusiveness of 'I,'" which we will discuss more fully in Chapter IV.

As he had at Cambridge, Ramsey immediately plunged into the life of Oxford. As a Fellow of Oriel College, he took a full role in the administrative, social and devotional life of the college, serving as Chairman of the Faculty of Theology, Librarian and Treasurer. He also served as Governor of Ripon Hall and as a member of the General Board of the Faculties of the University in 1951. Some have commented on his insistence on meticulous detail and of his persistence in the cause of justice. For instance, he appealed a parking fine for a spot outside Oriel College as unjust because others had been illegally parked but not fined.

Ramsey was an unusual teacher in every respect. He was always prepared not only for lectures, but also for seminars and tutorial and personal conferences. For everything he did he had a game plan and carried it out fully and with great effect. His lectures not only were gems of consistency and single-minded devotion to his own thesis concerning "disclosures," but also were positive attempts to move his hearers to examine their own beliefs and the contributions of other thinkers, including his own contributions. And, since he provided mimeographed notes to his students, they were able to fully reflect upon all of the philosophical and theological alternatives and make their own decision, a methodology which I have adopted in my teaching of philosophy of religion. Of course, there were times when Ramsey's attempts to adapt his central disclosure thesis to every problem area of religion seemed to be without the secure grounding which he assumed, yet he willingly accepted the consequences of critical analysis and comment. In grateful remembrance, many of his students recall his sincere humility as he considered the objector's case as fully and carefully as he had presented his own. Ramsey won the respect of both students and scholar-colleagues thereby.

His tenure at Oxford also was notable because of the numerous and prestigious lectureships with which Ramsey was honored. He was the Forwood Lecturer at the University of Liverpool in 1957 and published these lectures later under the title of *Freedom and Immortality* (1960). He was the Annual Theological Lecturer at Queen's University, Belfast, in 1960 and later published these lectures as *Religion and Science* (1964). He was the Frederick Denison Maurice Lecturer at King's College, London University in 1961–1962 and later published these lectures as *On Being Sure in Religion* (1963). He was the Whidden Lecturer, McMaster University, Hamilton, Canada in January, 1963, and published these lectures as *Models and Mystery* (1964). He was the Riddell Memorial Lecturer at the University of Newcastle upon Tyne in November, 1963, and published these lectures as *Christian Discourse* (1965). Other distinguished lectureships included the Alden-Tuthill Lectures on Theological Literacy at the University of Chicago in May, 1963, and the Zenos Lectures at McCormick Theological Seminary, Chicago in 1966, as well as numerous others.

Ramsey's fifteen years as Nolloth Professor of the Philosophy of the Christian Religion at Oxford were fruitful years in the arena of publications. His first (and many say his best) book was *Religious Language,* published in 1957 by the Student Christian Movement Press. A number of others followed: *The Reasonableness of Christianity,* a work of John Locke which Ramsey edited and for which he wrote a fine introduction (London, S. C. M. Press, 1960); *Prospect for Metaphysics,* which Ramsey edited and for which he prepared a paper (London, Allen & Unwin, 1961); *On Being Sure in Religion* (London, The Athlone Press, 1963); *Models and Mystery* (London, Oxford University Press, 1964); *Religion and Science* (London, S. P. C. K. Press, 1964); *Biology and Personality,* which Ramsey edited (Oxford, Basil Blackwell, 1965); *Christian Discourse* (London, Oxford University Press, 1965); and *Christian Ethics and Contemporary Philosophy,* which Ramsey edited and for which he prepared two articles and a reply (London, S. C. M. Press, 1966). In addition to this amazing list of publications Ramsey prepared, presented and had printed in countless journals literally hundreds of papers, articles, reviews and replies.

Ramsey himself characterized his tenure at Oxford as both "happy" and "productive." And regardless of what his colleagues at Oxford thought of Ramsey's philosophical theology, they were unanimous in praising his energy and productivity. And many also have paid tribute to his unusual empathy and warm, Christian good will and kindness. Indeed, Edwards in his biography of Ramsey quotes Professor Donald Evans, a former pupil, as saying that he was sincerely impressed by Ramsey's ability to encourage the potential in others and adds,

I often thought that if he had devoted less time and energy to me and countless others, and more to his own work, it would have been immeasurably better. One of the reasons why I wrote my *Religious Studies* articles about him was that I felt he had not done justice to himself.[5]

7. *Active Churchman and Enlightened Citizen*

Yet Ramsey was also very active during the Oxford years as a churchman and enlightened citizen. He accepted member-

ship on the Management Committee of the Warneford and
Park Hospitals in 1954 and served as its chairman in 1960.
With his usual energy and special skills and concerns he made
a noteworthy contribution to the ongoing program of that psy-
chiatric hospital. He also served as Examining Chaplain to
the Bishops of Portsmouth, Sheffield and Norwich and in 1964
accepted the Directorship of the Lambeth Diploma in Theology,
a program for Church of England laymen who were not able
to pursue a collegiate or seminary degree in theology.

However, it is in his enthusiastic and somewhat burdensome
commitment as a churchman-scholar, and more particularly
in the area of the church's social responsibility, that Ramsey
made a truly definitive and noteworthy contribution. His strong
interest in medical ethics and in the general relationship of
religion and science qualified him for membership on several
Church of England Commissions, e.g., on divine healing and
birth control. He was appointed by Archbishop Geoffrey Fisher
as advisor to a group of Anglican Bishops discussing "The
Family in Contemporary Society" at the Lambeth Conference
(of all Anglican Bishops worldwide) in 1958, and the document
which came from that section of the conference was a landmark
work. Ramsey later reprinted a paper which he had guided
to adoption in his book, *Christian Ethics and Contemporary
Philosophy.*

Ramsey's success in the Lambeth Conference endeavor
brought about his participation in similar reports on social
and ethical issues under consideration by the Church of England's Board for Social Responsibility, namely issues such
as: suicide, sterilization, punishment, abortion and decisions
about life and death. The reports prepared by the Board were
all sincere efforts to dissolve the ethical dilemmas involved
using all the tools and clarifying techniques of both philosophy
and the scientific method, and the application of decision-making procedures enlightened by Christian insights. All of the
reports were influential. The one on abortion received the broad-
est publicity and discussion, but the one on suicide, "Ought

Suicide to Be a Crime?" was named by the writers of the Suicide Act of 1960, in their accompanying White Paper, as influencing the framing of the act.

8. Bishop of Durham

It came as no great surprise to observers of the Church of England that Ramsey was considered in 1966 as the new Bishop of Durham. The combination of his reputation as a university scholar and philosophical theologian and his increasing contribution to the explanation and support of the social interests and responsibilities of the church highlighted his potential as a bishop of one of the outstanding Dioceses of the Church of England. Thus Ramsey became the ninetieth Bishop of Durham with his enthronement on 15 December 1966.

Ramsey was not the first scholar-churchman to be installed at the See of Durham. Before him were the Victorian Diocesans, Lightfoot and Wescott, but the one predecessor who bore the most striking similarities to Ramsey was Joseph Butler, who was both a metaphysician and an activist. Ramsey's enthronement sermon was a declaration of his intention to serve both the people and the interests of the region, but according to Edwards it was too long and too academic. Edwards' verdict is that it was inferior to Michael Ramsey's enthronement sermon of 1952. But he had openly embraced many of the important concerns of his somewhat depressed and disadvantaged county as well as the needs of the youth and the workingman. His words gave a clue to the all-too-brief ministry he would exercise of hope and warmth.

It was in this spirit and vision that Bishop Ramsey and Margretta took up residence in Auckland Castle outside of Durham and commented to friends that he loved it. Indeed, he eventually moved the Diocesan office from Durham to Auckland Castle. However, while the castle was somewhat remote from Durham, Ramsey was not remote from the people of his See. He truly loved his people, identified with them and

championed their causes. He was the speaker at the Durham
Miner's Gala and established the Tees-side Industrial Mission
to cite only two of his energetic efforts. He took up their causes
in the House of Lords, for instance, urging government help
to open factories in the northeast and demanding goverment
support in the cause of the aging.

There is little doubt about the respect and genuine affection
the Archbishop of Canterbury, Dr. Michael Ramsey, had for
Ian Ramsey. Interestingly enough, they were not related. The
Archbishop appointed Ramsey as chairman of a doctrinal commission to study the question of the mandatory subscription
of all Anglican clergymen to the Thirty-nine Articles of Religion, a Reformation statement of Protestant principles. The
commission report proposed that newly ordained clergy not
be obligated to "assent" to the Articles nor required to read
them publicly. The commission recommended that ordinands
profess their "firm and sincere belief in the faith set forth in
the Scriptures and in the Catholic Creeds, and [their] allegiance
to the doctrine of the Church of England."[6] The Archbishop
also made Ramsey Vice-Chairman of the section of the Lambeth
Conference concerned with "The Renewal of the Church in
Faith." It was in this role that he drafted its report and also
was editor of *Faith Alert,* a published summary of the section's
report. Ramsey also chaired the Church's Commission on Religious Education and edited their report, *The Fourth R,* which
was published in 1970. It too became an important document
in the educational system of Great Britain since it proposed
the reconciliation of Christians and secularists in the development of a curriculum for the effective teaching of religion in
British schools.

Bishop Ramsey also continued his interest in the field of
religion and medicine. He had enthusiastically helped to organize the Institute of Religion and Medicine in 1964 and, as
Bishop of Durham, he became its chairman in 1971. He devoted
increasing time and energy to engagements on behalf of the
cause of bringing together clergy and members of the health-

care professions to consider both the theological and medical aspects of the healing process. His efforts led the way to a significant expansion of the work and influence of the Institute in every part of Britain. Ramsey also wrote prefaces to both volumes of *Religion and Medicine* sponsored by the Institute.

The Bishop of Durham also accepted the Chairmanship of the British Broadcasting Corporation's Central Religious Advisory Committee in 1970. Ramsey was a "natural" to head the CRAC, for he was especially good at getting diverse peoples and interests to clarify their positions and to accept the views of disagreeing opponents. Colleagues testify that at the first meeting of CRAC in March, 1971, he had accomplished a minor miracle in achieving a unanimity between the BBC and the Independent Broadcasting Association on time allotments for religious television. Actually, Bishop Ramsey chaired only three meetings. He had suffered a heart attack in the spring of 1972, Easter Eve to be precise. Then after a summer of convalescence and a very light schedule for September, he traveled to London for a meeting of CRAC on 6 October 1972. Unfortunately the day of this meeting was to be the last day of Ian Ramsey's life. He died shortly after the meeting at the age of fifty-seven.

9. *Three Friendly Assessments*

My own experience with Ramsey can be summed up in one word—unforgettable. Following our meeting at the Philadelphia Divinity School, he surprised me by his favorable comments on my contributions to the discussions which followed his lectures, and by his invitation to join him at Oxford for a term to explore more thoroughly some of the questions we had briefly confronted. His invitation led to an Episcopal Church Fellowship at Oxford in the Trinity Term of 1964 and to the beginning of a warm relationship which was an inspiring source of personal motivation and productivity in my academic and writing career. No doubt I was one of the many who added to Ramsey's overcrowded schedule and myriad personal concerns. However, he never failed to answer a letter promptly and pick up the personal interests and matters where he had left off in the previous epistle. Further, he took the time to read my manuscripts and to return them promptly, covered with numerous notations and criticisms in his own careful style and inimitable small, tight handwriting. Ramsey had that special quality of making everyone feel important and his or her ideas worthy. He was one savant who was at the same time wise and caring. In this respect Ramsey towered over his peers—scholars and churchmen alike.

Edwards is quite critical of Ramsey's zealous stewardship of his time and energy, and thus, in the end, of Bishop Ramsey's episcopal efforts. Edwards admits that Ramsey was a layman's bishop who saw clearly the needs of people and gladly gave them his sympathy and his energy. However, Edwards questions Ramsey's administrative abilities, more specifically his lack of overall strategy and policy and his inability to delegate authority. Edwards also calls attention to Ramsey's failure to follow up his social pronouncements and reforms with the programs to make them possible. No doubt these criticisms can be laid at the foot of the basic concern that Ramsey had so much difficulty organizing his own work and shepherding his own energies and physical resources that in the end his lack of concern for the effective stewardship of time and strength tragically cut short a fruitful career as philosopher, theologian and churchman.

The address of Michael Ramsey, Archbishop of Canterbury, at the memorial service for Ian Ramsey at St. Margaret's, Westminster on Friday, 17 November 1972, supports to some degree Edwards' assessment. However, since it is a fitting tribute to a most able and wonderful man, it will serve as an appropriate conclusion to this chapter.

Three of Durham's great bishops were buried in the lovely medieval chapel of Auckland Castle: Cosin, Lightfoot, Westcott; and it is fitting that the ashes of Ian Ramsey are to lie near to them. It will not be surprising if history comes to remember Brooke Foss Westcott and Ian Ramsey as the two bishops who made the biggest impact upon the Durham community.

It is never easy to speak about a dear friend or a great man, and it is doubly hard to speak about one who was both. I have known other men who had something of Ian's winning warmth of heart and others who had Ian's liveliness of mind; but I have never known one in whom the warm heart and the lively mind were so completely of one piece. That was the secret of his influence as a theologian. He cared intensely that theology should listen to other disciplines if it is to have something intelligible to say in the contemporary scene. He cared no less that those who speak about Christian faith should do so with sensitivity to the many who find faith hard or incredible. These gifts made Ian Ramsey nearly unique amongst the theologians of our time in winning the attention and respect of people trained in other kinds of mental discipline. And for Ian this outreach on the frontiers of faith could never be an intellectual process alone. It meant outgoing friendship with people of many professions, a ceaseless engagement of heart and mind alike, a ceaseless giving of himself.

So when Ian left the academic life of Oxford for the very different tasks of a Bishop of Durham there was, for all the vast change of scene, a striking continuity of work and character. In Durham it was quickly apparent that he cared greatly about the community and its problems and was thinking vigorously about them. Those who worked in the mines and the shipyards, trades—unionists and managers alike, those who took part in local government or education or medicine or the social services, saw in the bishop one who understood and cared, with a concern for people as well as for ideas and causes. So there was a renewal in a fresh form of the historic link between the see of Durham and the community, for Ian had a sense of the past as well as the present, and he was never happier than when he welcomed crowds of visitors to the bishop's historic home and showed them the memorials of his great predecessors.

Inevitably Ian Ramsey's leadership was reaching far beyond his own diocese. The work of the Doctrine Commission, the production of the report on education entitled *The Fourth R*, the work of other groups of his own creation, a succession of speeches in the House of Lords made with the weight of considerable knowledge—amid all this his impact as a Christian leader was growing, and it was a leadership of a kind which no one else could give. But a frightening problem began to appear.

Is it possible for one man to lead the pastoral work of a diocese with its outreach to the community and at the same time to be taking part in national affairs and at the same time also to conserve the work of study, reading, thought, and teaching? Not many bishops have tried to combine these three roles at once, and those who have tried know that survival is only possible if there is a rigorous discipline in excluding things which do not matter and limiting painfully the things which do. Alas, it was impossible for Ian to admit the advice and experience of those who know something of the problem, because it had become a deep and inseparable part of his character never to say "no." And in the office which he held never to say "no" means before long to lose the power of discrimination and to be living in a whirl of mental and physical movement. The whirl became the whirlwind which swept Ian, like Elijah of old, to Paradise.

Yet perhaps if it were otherwise Ian would not be Ian. Perhaps the saying of "no" to any request of a fellow human being and the planning of priorities for himself were impossible for one to whom any incidental encounter, any person met, could be a thrilling disclosure, a bursting forth of one of God's secrets. Such was the man, with mind and heart ceaselessly engaged with truth and ready for truth to break out anywhere in a blaze of glory. That was the Ian God gave to us, and we are thanking God today for one of the best of his gifts that we have known, a gift not like any other. Our loving prayers surround Ian's brave family at this time, and for Ian we pray that he will now have the vision which our Savior promised to the pure in heart.[7]

10. A Look Ahead

With this all-too-brief biographical survey of the life of Ian Ramsey, we will turn in succeeding chapters to the major components of the subtitle of this volume: "Philosophical Theology in the Empiricist, Analytical Mode." In Chapter II we will examine both the classical and contemporary interpretations of empiricism. In Chapter III we will inquire into the meanings and expressions of empirical theology as well as the philosophical analyses of theological language. In Chapter IV we will investigate what it means to call one's self a "Christian empiricist," and more specifically about how Ramsey's theories supply meaning and sense to religious discourse. And finally in Chapter V we will confront some criticisms and replies and assess Ramsey and his empiricist, analytical mode of approaching philosophical theology.

II. EMPIRICAL PHILOSOPHY:
Classical and Contemporary

A. Introduction

To understand more fully Ramsey's announced "Christian empiricism," it is necessary to review and have an understanding of empirical philosophy in general; of both its classical and contemporary manifestations and practitioners. This chapter will consider briefly but precisely the philosophical source of empiricism and note the more influential teachings of the British philosophers responsible for its classical statement—namely Francis Bacon, Thomas Hobbes, John Locke, George Berkeley and David Hume.

We will also survey the later developments of empiricism, first under the heading of the earliest major American philosophical contribution, the radical empiricism of William James and John Dewey, and second under the heading of logical empiricism which had its expression in the work of British and continental philosophers, chief of which were G. E. Moore, Bertrand Russell, the members of the Vienna Circle, Ludwig Wittgenstein, A. J. Ayer and Gilbert Ryle. The survey will show the movement within contemporary empirical philosophy from rigid positivism and the rejection of metaphysics, ethics and religion to conceptual or language analysis which expanded the concerns of empirical philosophy to include a broader interest in every major problem with which man wrestles for meaning and solutions.

B. Classical Empiricism

Historically, empirical philosophy had its origin in sixteenth-century England, although some medieval scholars, namely Roger Bacon and Robert Grosseteste, had considered more experimental methods in the sciences. The word empirical (see empiric and empiricism) comes from the Greek word *empeirikos*, which means "experienced," from the word *empeiria* meaning "experience" (from the prefix *en*, literally "in," and *peira*, literally "trial" or "experiment"). Thus empirical philosophy is founded on the theory that sense experience is the only source of knowledge, and in this usage "experience," from its Latin source *experientia*, means literally "test" or "trial." Empiricists, from the beginning, have insisted that what we know is verified by observation and by experiment with existential reference to some object. Further, they hold that such knowledge is presented in a posteriori propositions, or statements that follow or are the consequence of experience. Some empirical philosophers contend that such propositions alone guarantee certainty of knowledge. Empiricists regard as unscientific a priori propositions or judgments (concepts acquired "prior to" or without experience) and innate ideas or knowledge, as well as most metaphysical thought. In the scientific arena, empirical refers to that part of the scientific method which provides for the development of a hypothesis into a law.

The true founder of British empirical philosophy was Francis Bacon (1561–1626), who reformed both philosophy and science by his challenge of both Platonism and Aristotelianism and by his proclamation of a new method in the sciences. Bacon boasted, "I have taken all knowledge to be my province," and set out to accomplish this boast in his projected "Great Instauration," of which he completed only two parts: a survey of existing knowledge and the sciences in his book, *Dignity and Advancement of the Sciences* (1605); and a critique of Aristotle's method with the elaboration of a new method for inquiry in his book, *Novum Organum* (1620). He criticized both a priori reasoning and the deductive method as ways to certain truth or new discovery, and advocated a purely experimental method based on observations of particulars and moving by the inductive method to general truth and scientific generalization.

In Aphorisms 19, 22 and 24 of his *First Book of Aphorisms*, Bacon published his criticism of the science of the ancients. According to Bacon there are only two methods scientific inquiry can employ in discovering truth. One way begins with the most general axioms, without any serious attempt to base these principles on experience. Proceeding deductively, this first method assumes the truth of its general principles and goes on to derive more specific axioms. Bacon complains that this method, all too prevalent in Aristotle's treatises, still held sway in his own day. The other method would insist upon a careful empirical inspection of particulars as the basis upon which principles are to be constructed. The most general principles would be arrived at last since their soundness would depend on a gradual and rigorous marshalling of ever wider arrays of facts. This way, Bacon urges, is "the true way, but as yet untried . . ." (Aph. 19). Since the first method is content merely to "just glance at experiment and particulars in passing" (Aph. 22) and to derive other axioms solely through deductive argumentation, it cannot possibly be fruitful in discovering the intricacies of nature, the disclosure of which makes possible new works of invention and power. The subtlety of nature, Bacon reminds us, is far greater than the most subtle of purely deductive arguments. On the other hand, inductively established principles, based as they are upon experiment and attention to particulars, build into scientific inquiry the capacity for the discovery of new facts. (Aph. 24)[1]

Yet, while Bacon's announced goal of "the total reconstruction of . . . all human knowledge" was unashamedly immodest, nevertheless he did weaken the hold of scholasticism on British thinkers and made possible the advent of the later empiricists who revolutionalized philosophy in the seventeenth and eighteenth centuries. Bacon also insisted on the distinction of science from theology arguing that science had been retarded by being forced to abide by theological methods. Still he was not irreligious and advised ". . . a little philosophy inclineth man's mind to atheism, but depth in philosophy bringeth men's mind about to religion."[2] Nevertheless he did demand that science must observe and interpret the facts of nature as inquiry perceives them. The importance and influence of Francis Bacon is confirmed by John Dewey, who devoted an entire chapter to Bacon, naming him as one who exemplified the new way of philosophy anchored in nature and the experience of man.

Thomas Hobbes (1588–1679) was a colleague of and a worthy successor to Bacon. Indeed, Hobbes translated some of Bacon's essays into Latin. Yet, Hobbes seemed much more interested in the physics of Galileo, who, said Hobbes, "opened . . . the gate of natural knowledge universal, which is the knowledge of the nature of motion."[3] Still, Hobbes turned ultimately to geometry, and his zeal for and confidence in geometric methods resulted in a break with Baconian inductive methods and simple observation. On this break Hobbes remarked, "Experience concludeth nothing universally."[4] And with this rejoinder Hobbes joined the continental philosophers who used geometry to find the key to the study of nature.

Yet, in spite of Hobbes' conversion to geometric procedures, he remained a materialist and a skeptic. He attacked the scholastic philosophers no less rigorously than Bacon, rejecting their abstractions in traditional metaphysics as meaningless and without any significance, arguing that words have meaning only when they are produced by sensation or feeling. All our thoughts, according to Hobbes, originate either totally or partially in our sense organs. Further, Hobbes' prescription that philosophy follow the lead of geometry in providing clear definitions and empirical reference is a forecast of the critical analyses and pronouncements of the logical positivists and empiricists of the recent past. His view that all existence, including experience and knowledge, is mechanical was based on the assumption that all bodies (matter, human and political) are involved in motion and that all events and their causes are produced by that motion. Therefore, for Hobbes, mind is a mechanical activity in the body, a sense organ, which receives our impressions of things as "phantasms" (ideas of the motions of matter and change), the motion of which gives rise to "imagination" (any experience prompting mental images).

For Hobbes, no incorporeal substances existed, e.g., spirit of God. He accepted the idea of God, if that God, like other persons, could be said to be material. Hobbes also accepted no teleology (or final causes) in his materialist cosmology, although the second part of *Leviathan* is a full and sometimes tedious discussion "Of a Christian Commonwealth" and "Of the Kingdom of Darkness." Two of Hobbes' more familiar pronouncements on religion and the language of religion occur in the context of his humanist "manifesto" and his account of visions or personal revelations. Since, suggests Hobbes, all the signs and fruits of religion are exhibited by and through human beings only, without a doubt man only must be the "seed of religion."[5] Hobbes' rejection of the supernatural or of any intervention of an immaterial Spirit in human life leads him to regard alleged personal revelations or visions as only instances of an individual dreaming that God spoke to him.[6]

Hobbes' pronouncement on the importance of the analysis of language sounds almost contemporary. He wrote:

Seeing that *truth* consisteth in the right ordering of names in our affirmations, a man that seeketh precise *truth* had need to remember what every name he uses stands for, and to place it accordingly. . . . By this it appears how necessary it is for any man that aspires to true Knowledge to examine the Definitions of former Authors, and either to correct them . . . or to make them himself. For the errors of Definition multiply themselves, according as the reckoning proceeds; and lead men into absurdities. . . .[7]

With similar criticisms and recommendations, Hobbes helped Bacon to alter the course of philosophy with the consistent application of the methods of science to the study of nature, human nature and moral (and political) behavior. His epistemological and other explanations may be novel and wrongheaded, but they were revolutionary and influential in the history of philosophy.

John Locke (1632–1704) inherited the task of developing a philosophical system based on experience and the empirical method begun by Bacon. Locke's declared goal was more modest than Bacon's. As he described it in the "Epistle to the Reader" in his *Essay on Human Understanding*,

It is ambition enough to be employed . . . in clearing the ground a little, and removing some of the rubbish that lies in the way to knowledge. . . . Vague and insignificant forms of speech, and abuse of language, have so long passed for mysteries of science; and hard or misapplied words, with little or no meaning, have [been] . . . mistaken for deep learning. . . .[8]

In his *Essay*, Locke provided the foundation for empirical philosophy by inquiring into the origin, certainty and extent of human knowledge and thus provided a new method of attack on the so-called "epistemological problem." He set out his method in the introduction very carefully.

First. I shall inquire into the original of those ideas, notions, or whatever else you please to call them, which a man observes, and is conscious to himself he has in his mind; and the ways whereby the understanding comes to be furnished with them.

Secondly. I shall endeavour to show what knowledge the understanding hath by those ideas, and the certainty, evidence, and extent of it.

Thirdly. I shall make some inquiry into the nature and grounds of faith or opinion; whereby I mean, that assent which we give to any proposition as true, of whose truth yet we have no certain knowledge: and here we shall have occasion to examine the reasons and degrees of assent.[9]

He systematically refutes the doctrines of the rationalists, such as: innate ideas, self-evident or intuited knowledge, universal principles (Do unto others as you would have them do to you) and a priori propositions and knowledge. In his *Essay*, Locke establishes experience alone as the basis of knowledge. Indeed, Locke's philosophy is literally a philosophy of common sense as he argues that all our ideas come either from sensation or reflection. Locke suggests that the human mind is like a sheet of white or blank paper[10] on which experience inscribes ideas. Such ideas are generated by objects which we experience and which come to our minds through sensation or observation or reflection by "the internal operations of our minds." Locke's primitive empiricism brings to mind the old Aristotelian (and scholastic) slogan, "There is nothing in the mind which has not previously been in the senses."

On the subject of knowledge in general, Locke comments:

> Knowledge then seems to me to be nothing but the perception of the connection of and agreement, or disagreement and repugnancy, of any of our ideas. In this alone it consists. Where this perception is, there is knowledge; and where it is not, there, though we may fancy, guess, or believe, yet we always come short of knowledge.[11]

For Locke, then, knowledge can extend only as far as we have ideas. More specifically, knowledge must be restricted exclusively to the perceptions of the relations between ideas. These perceptions may be of three sorts, according to Locke. (1) The perception may consist of the immediate comparison of any two ideas, in which case it is an intuition. (2) The perception, by employing other ideas, may be concerned with exhibiting the agreement or disagreement of ideas. Locke calls this operation a perception of reason. And (3) Locke reserves the term "sensation" for the most basic kind of perception, "perceiving the existence of particular things."[12]

In explaining the scope of religious knowledge, Locke distinguishes between those propositions which are "above, contrary and according to reason." The propositions which accord with reason may be ultimately traced back to sensation and reflection. Their truth or at least the probability of their being true may then be established by demonstrating their connection to experience. Propositions which are above reason cannot be so derived from sensation or reflection. Any propositions which are inconsistent with or contradict our clear and distinct ideas are contrary to reason. Accordingly, for Locke, the existence of one God is a rational proposition, the proposition which asserts the existence of more than one God is contrary to reason, and the claim that the dead may be resurrected is above reason.[13] According to Locke, we are able to have certain knowledge of the existence of God. His argument demonstrating the existence of God begins with what is experiential and then goes on to assert that the character of this conditional experience necessitates the existence of God, an unconditional Being. Thus, Locke argues, man perceives that he himself is finite and did not exist at some time in the past. One may then infer that should the absence of all finite beings be contemplated, then it is clear that nothing would exist, since nothing cannot produce a being. Therefore, the argument concludes, since there are finite beings, there must exist from all eternity an infinite, unconditioned being, namely God, who is the ultimate cause of all that is. Locke insists that " . . . we have a more certain knowledge of the existence of a God, than of anything our senses have not immediately discovered to us."[14]

Locke's most helpful contribution to the philosophy of religion lies in his distinction between reason and faith:

> *Reason* therefore here, as contradistinguished to faith, I take to be the discovery of the certainty or probability of such propositions or truths,

which the mind arrives at by deductions made from such ideas which it has got by the use of its natural faculties, viz, by sensation or reflection.

Faith, on the other side, is the assent to any proposition, not thus made out by the deductions of reason, but upon the credit of the proposer, as coming from God in some extraordinary way of communication. This way of discovering truths to men we call *revelation.* [15]

Yet for Locke, "reason must be our last judge and guide,"[16] and faith must not be "contradictory to our clear intuitive knowledge."[17]

The influence of Locke is inestimable. He is the founder of modern epistemology who asked the proper questions and suggested the appropriate methods of inquiry into the scope and limitations of the human mind. Locke also was the voice of political liberalism, whose views on equality and natural rights found their way into the U.S. Constitution. But his early thoughts on the critical analysis of language, such as those quoted by A. G. N. Flew in his Introduction to *Essays on Logic and Language* (see p. 66 for the quotation), indicate the depth of his contribution to the ongoing logical empiricist tradition within contemporary philosophy.

George Berkeley (1685–1753) was one of the staunchest of the classical empirical philosophers, yet paradoxically he was also a religious idealist, theologian and a Church of England cleric who was Bishop of Cloyne, Ireland. Interestingly, Berkeley was somewhat of a hero to Ian T. Ramsey. Indeed, there are several superficial similarities between their beliefs and teachings. Berkeley is responsible for the famous slogan for empiricism, *esse est percipi,* which means "to be is to be perceived," and which tersely represents the empirical claim that all knowledge depends on actual sensory experiences—thus perceptions. In his *A Treatise Concerning the Principles of Human Knowledge* he wrote:

It is indeed an opinion strangely prevailing amongst men, that houses, mountains, rivers, and in a word all sensible objects, have an existence, natural or real, distinct from their being perceived by the understanding.

. . . For, what are the fore-mentioned objects but the things we perceive by sense? and what do we perceive besides our own ideas or sensations? and is it not plainly repugnant that any one of these, or any combination of them, should exist unperceived?[18]

Further, Berkeley insisted we know nothing except the ideas of our perceiving mind, which is the same as to claim that we know nothing except as related to a mind—ours or God's. Thus ultimately it is God from whom all reality is perceived as presented to our minds. Therefore reality is simply an expression of divine thought. Berkeley's summary slogan is *esse est percipi et percipers,* which means "being is percepts and perceivers."

Berkeley was at once both the heir and the critic of John Locke. At the very outset of his *Treatise,* Berkeley critically sums up what he takes to be the essential meaning of Locke's empiricism. Names like "apple," "stone," "brook," or the names of any other objects of sensation refer to a collection of sensible qualities such as color, taste, smell and consistency which are observed to occur together. Actually, Berkeley followed Locke's empirical method more precisely than Locke. Berkeley was critical of Locke's doctrine of abstract ideas and restricted his own use of "idea" to perception and imagery, eliminating strictly mental concepts. He insisted that no abstract idea can be deduced from concrete experience. Indeed, in his Introduction to *A Treatise,* he notes that abstract and merely verbal concepts serve no other purpose than to obstruct and obscure genuine scientific inquiry. Berkeley then resolves to confine his thoughts only to those ideas of which he has a "clear and adequate"[19] perception.

Berkeley's rigid empiricism was aimed against materialism, a doctrine which he also campaigned against as a churchman. He held that since all percepts are those of a perceiving mind, a material reality is inconceivable, a meaningless concept. Berkeley argued "that all the . . . furniture of the earth [has] not any subsistence without a mind, . . . or else . . . the mind of some Eternal Spirit. . . . [Thus] it follows there is not any other substance than *Spirit,* or that which perceives."[20]

It was in this way that Berkeley arrived at the most paradoxical point of his empirical philosophy, *viz.,* that since knowledge of the world as a totality can only be perceived by mind, it follows that the reality of the world in its entirety is perceived only by God. Actually, Berkeley's argument for the existence of God is teleological with a cosmological twist. He argued that the design exhibited in Nature implies a designer who must be God. Thus, when we take into account how all aspects of the universe comprise a harmonious order—how on the macrocosmic scale the universe exhibits a wondrous beauty and perfection, and how on the microcosmic scale the most intricate small parts are built into the most exquisite contrivances, and above all how the system of living things is ordered by the laws of pain, pleasure and instincts—it is apparent that the universe manifests an infinite and superordinate Intelligence, God, an Infinitely Wise, Good, and Perfect Spirit "who works all in all" and "by whom all things consist."[21] Berkeley's apologetic against materialism and skepticism may or may not have been successful; nevertheless his influence as an empirical philosopher secured a lasting fame. David Hume, Berkeley's philosophic successor, spoke of Berkeley as "a great philosopher [who] has asserted that all general ideas are nothing but particular ones . . . I look upon this to be one of the greatest and most valuable discoveries that has been made . . . in the republic of letters."[22] Ramsey pays his tribute to Berkeley in his book *Models for Divine Activity,* noting that "George Berkeley in an earlier day criticized the 'abstracted metaphysics' which led to theological 'wire-drawing' and pointed to a broadened empiricism as the cure."[23] And Berkeley himself called attention to his relevance to contemporary analytic philosophy by emphasizing the importance of language analysis. "We need only draw the curtain of words, to hold the fairest tree of knowledge, whose fruit is excellent, and within the reach of our hand."[24]

David Hume (1711–1776) is generally named as the greatest British philosopher, the most consistent empiricist who "pushed empiricism to its logical consequences"—skepticism. He is appropriately regarded as the spiritual father of modern logical empiricism, progenitor of both positivism and analytic philosophy. Samuel Enoch Stumpf, a contemporary historian of philosophy, summarized Hume's uniqueness saying that it was Hume who "concluded that if we take seriously the premise that all our ideas come from experience, we must accept the limits to knowledge that this . . . forces upon us, no matter what our customary beliefs suggest,"[25] e.g., reality and causality.

Hume's general thesis is stated in his book, *A Treatise of Human Nature: "That all our simple ideas in their first appearance, are derived from simple impressions, which are correspondent to them, and which they exactly represent."*[26] For Hume, all knowledge is gained only from sense and experience through perceptions or impressions (original experiences of both sensations and emotions) and ideas ("faint images" of impressions in our thought). Indeed, without impressions there could be no ideas. Hume explained that "Every idea is copied from some preceding impression or sentiment; and where we cannot find any impression, we may be certain that there is no idea."[27]

Based on this empirical foundation, Hume expressed his criterion for meaning boldly: ". . . we need but inquire, *from what impression is that supposed idea derived?* And if it be impossible to assign any, this will serve to confirm our suspicion [that a philosophical term is employed without any meaning or idea]."[28] Therefore, Hume concludes, an idea which cannot trace its origin to an impression is nonsense. Hume's analysis of causality is a forceful application of his criterion of meaning. When asked to certify that X is the cause of Y, former philosophers have attempted it in many ways, i.e., as a force in nature. Hume denied this. He asks, "From what impression is the idea of causality derived?" Hume answers "None!" He then points out that cause and effect are supported only by the constant conjunction (connection) or sequence (contiguity) and succession of ideas which merely suggest causal association, concluded on a principle of custom or habit. The "doctrine" of cause and effect therefore becomes for Hume little more than a psychological phenomenon and since no objective impression supports our belief, it is nothing but a prejudice (albeit a necessary one). Hume's conclusion is quite emphatic. He says:

> Upon the whole, necessity is something that exists in the mind, not in objects; nor is it possible for us ever to form the most distant idea of it, considered as a quality in bodies. Either we have no idea of necessity, or necessity is nothing but that determination of the thought to pass from causes to effects, and from effects to causes, according to their experienced union.[29]

The extension of his criterion for meaning to other ideas, e.g., to self, substance and God, developed similar analyses and skeptical conclusions. Hume denied that we can have any idea of self based on impressions. What we can know of personal identity is "nothing but a bundle or collection of different perceptions," with the mind "a kind of theatre where several perceptions successively make their appearance."[30] Thus, according to Hume, we never have a perception of the soul or self as an enduring subject underlying our perceptions. Similarly Hume denies, with Berkeley, the idea of substance, arguing that "We have . . . no idea of substance, distinct from that of a collection of particular qualities, nor have we any other meaning when we talk of it."[31] Thus, for Hume, the reality of substance (of self or objects) is no more than an attempt to explain the connection in the mind between repeated perceptions.

It was inevitable that his criterion of meaning would lead to religious skepticism. In his *Inquiry*, Hume set the tone of his critique.

> If we take in our hand any volume—of divinity or school metaphysics, for instance—let us ask, *Does it contain any abstract reasoning concerning*

quantity or number? No. *Does it contain any experimental reasoning concerning matter or fact and existence?* No. Commit it then to the flames, for it can contain nothing but sophistry and illusion.[32]

Further, Hume argues, "No new fact can ever be inferred from the religious hypothesis, no event foreseen or foretold, no reward or punishment expected or dreaded, beyond what is already known by practice and observation."[33] In general, therefore, Hume's philosophy of religion was concerned mostly with exposing the fallacies involved in proving the existence of God, the efficacy of miracles and the possibility of immortality, along with an effort to show how religious ideas developed from human experience without supernatural intervention.

Hume offered critiques of the major arguments for the existence of God. While he admits that the argument from design or teleology sounds plausible—that the order in the universe suggests an orderer (or designer), Hume found William Paley's analogy of the watch found on a deserted island and its prescribed watchmaker unconvincing. Hume points out that such order could be accounted for in terms of a chance process or by natural selection. And above all the analogy of watch/watchmaker to universe/creator—God is both ambiguous and uncertain because the subject of universe and its creator lies beyond the scope of human experience.

Hume also notes problems with both the ontological argument (the existence of God is self-evident) and the cosmological argument (God exists as everything's first cause). First, the ontological argument relies on a priori "proof" by definition (which is to say that it depends on a point of logic or prior assumptions); such proof Hume calls absurd. No matter of fact, Hume points out, can be demonstrated through purely logical or a priori argumentation. No assertion is logically necessary and thus demonstrable unless its contrary would be self-contradictory. Every matter of fact which is conceivable may be conceived of as nonexistent without involving one in any logical contradiction. Thus, there is no being the nonexistence of which implies a contradiction. Consequently, as far as Hume is concerned, this argument decisively shows that there is no being, including God's, whose existence is demonstrable.[34]

Second, since the cosmological argument relies on the idea of causality, Hume's original criticism and denial applies. And while Hume admits "that the cause or causes of order in the universe probably bear some . . . analogy to human intelligence . . . ,"[35] still we can have no experience (impression) of either the universe or cause, and therefore we can have no sensible idea.

Finally, Hume uses the classical case of evil as a reason to doubt the existence of the theist's God. He insists that Epicurus' old questions are yet unanswered. "Is he willing to prevent evil, but not able? then is he impotent. Is he able, but not willing? then is he malevolent. Is he both able and willing? whence then is evil?"[36] And, because analogies between God and man on such qualities as omnipotence, benevolence, infinite love, etc., are not helpful (Hume would say impossible), holding to the existence of God in the face of experienced evil is against both reason and experience. Hume concludes that the reasoning underlying Epicurus' queries is "so short, so clear, and so decisive" that nothing can shake its solidarity. The only recourse left, suggests Hume, would be to propose that the theological problem raised by the existence of evil exceeds the capacity of human understanding and all the common measures of validity which are employed in any human inquiry.[37]

It is quite obvious that Hume's radical skepticism as the result of his rigorous empirical philosophy undermined his religious convictions. In his conclusion to *The Natural History of Religion*, Hume wrote, "The whole is a riddle, an enigma, an inexplicable mystery. Doubt, uncertainty, suspense of judgment appear the only result of our most accurate scrutiny, concerning this subject."[38] And in his conclusion to Book I of *A Treatise*, Hume summed up his own evaluation of "this philosophical melancholy."

I dine, I play a game of backgammon, I converse, and am merry with my friends; and when, after three or four hours' amusement, I would return to these speculations, they appear cold, and strained, and ridiculous, that I cannot find in my heart to enter into them any further.[39]

Hume's influence has been beyond description. The Enlightenment German philosopher, Immanuel Kant, credits Hume with "awakening him from his dogmatic slumber." John Stuart Mill's famous essays in logic, ethics and political philosophy published over a century later carry on the spirit of Hume's work. Indeed, A. J. Ayer notes "that the best part of . . . Mill's work consists in development of the analyses carried out by Hume."[40] And Ayer further argues that Hume was a practitioner of the art of philosophical analysis and points out Hume's rejection of metaphysics as well as his clever analysis of causality. And with both positions Ayer is in hearty agreement. (See pp. 60–62).

C. Contemporary Empiricism

1. Radical Empiricism—Hume's heirs in the United States

Radical empiricism is a name coined by William James (1842–1910) to describe the doctrine that experience is the ultimate criterion of reality in knowledge. James accepted Hume's dictum that ideas are reducible to sensations, but insisted that statements about sensations are as much matters of experience as the things experienced. Thus James, under the influence of Hume and his successors, notably J. S. Mill and his own contemporary Charles Sanders Peirce, developed and made popular a form of contemporary empiricism under the new title of "pragmatism." James' empirical philosophy maintains both important classical criteria of empiricism: that ideas are reducible to sensations (impressions), and that experience is the criterion (source of knowledge). James discusses his choice of empiricism as the adoption of a temperament, of a "tough-minded" ("going by 'facts' ") attitude as compared to a "tender-minded" ("going by 'principles' ") attitude of rationalism.[41]

James was so aware of the influence of Mill that he dedicated *Pragmatism* to the positivist, " . . . from whom I first learned the pragmatic openness of mind and whom my fancy likes to picture as our leader were he alive to-day."[42] And James' tribute is well deserved, for it was Mill who best described the rigor of positivism. According to Mill, knowledge must restrict itself to describing the various relations between phenomena. This knowledge must always be relative in character since it will be concerned only with the relation of facts to other facts in terms of either succession or similitude. For Mill, science, then, cannot provide an understanding of the essence or ultimate causes, either efficient or final, of phenomena. Insofar as science teaches us about laws governing the relations between phenomena, these scientific laws merely describe the constant sequences and resemblances between phenomena, which in fact we do observe regularly.[43]

However, it was the influence on James of Peirce's "semantical agnosticism" which moved James to the fullest expression of pragmatism and thus of radical empiricism. Peirce had pioneered what he called the pragmatic theory of meaning, developing the word from the Greek word *pragma*, meaning "things done," acts or deeds. Peirce held that meaning is not derived by intuition, privately, but by experiment (or operation), publicly, by the effects or consequences. And, he insisted, if experience or operation fails to supply meaning, the statement is nonsense. In a now-famous article, "How to Make Our Ideas Clear," Peirce pointed out that "our idea of anything *is* our idea of its sensible effects . . . [And] it is absurd to say that thought has any meaning unrelated to its . . . function." Based on this, Peirce offered a "rule." "Consider what effects, which might conceivably have practical bearings, we conceive the object of our conception to have. Then, our conception of these effects is the whole of our conception of the object."[44]

James described his radical empiricism in the preface to

his book *The Meaning of Truth* in terms of three claims, the first of which he calls a "postulate," the second a "statement of fact," and the third a "generalized conclusion" which follows from the first two claims. The postulate states "that the only things that shall be debatable among philosophers shall be things definable in terms drawn from experience." The statement of fact proposes that the conjunctive and disjunctive relations between things are just as much a part of "direct particular experience" as the things themselves. Radical empiricism then proposes as a general conclusion that experience is self-referential, contains within it its own continuous structure, and therefore is in need of no "extraneous trans-empirical connective support."[45] Actually, James' empiricism differed from Hume's mostly due to James' view of relations. James rejected the atomistic view of experience he detected in Hume's as well as Kant's epistemology. For James, experience is either a collection of discrete impressions or a mass of sense representations needing systematizing by association of ideas (Hume) or categories (Kant).

In many ways pragmatism did accomplish the synthesis between British empiricism, positivism, utilitarianism, science and rational methodology while rejecting both idealism and rationalism. As James insists, there are no world formulae, no dogmas or doctrines, "It is a method only."[46] James goes on to explain that adopting the pragmatic method means that every answer, every proposed general concept about the nature of things, such as the Absolute, for example, must be regarded as provisional and never as closing the inquiry. Each concept must establish its "cash value" in terms of its capacity to illumine and further amplify the stream of experience from which it first arose. Thus, according to James, theories are not so much solutions as a "program for more work" or "instruments" which indicate the way existing realities may be changed.[47] James also enunciates the pragmatic theory of truth, which was revolutionary in its conception of the nature of truth as instrumental. For James "truth" meant ". . . nothing but this, *that ideas*

(*which themselves are but parts of our experience*) *become true
just in so far as they help us to get into satisfactory relations
with other parts of our experience.*"[48]

James criticises "old fashioned theism" and the more liberal,
immanent pantheism popular at his time for their remoteness
and abstractness. He commends pragmatism, since as he said,
". . . she is . . ."

> Interested in no conclusions but those which our minds and our experi-
> ences work out together, she has no *a priori* prejudices against theology.
> *If theological ideas prove to have a value for concrete life, they will be
> true, for pragmatism, in the sense of being good for so much. For how
> much more they are true, will depend entirely on their relations to the
> other truths that also have to be acknowledged.*[49]

James has been called a voluntarist (religious faith is "volun-
tarily" accepted and willed) in his explanation of religious
knowledge and language. His book *The Will to Believe* argues
that questions of faith are of such momentous import that we
are forced to consider all the live options possible to us. And
we dare not wait until all the evidence is in before deciding.
He recommends that "*Our passional nature . . . must decide*
[or] *risk losing the truth.*"[50] And further, James prescribes that
we join him in "radically saying . . . that we have the right
to believe at our own risk any hypothesis that is live enough
to tempt our will."[51]

It is obvious that James was not simply an imitator of the
British empiricists, he was a major empirical philosopher in
his own right. And while his pragmatism was anticipated by
Peirce and revised by John Dewey, James was the key thinker
and writer in the pragmatist movement. James was an excellent
craftsman whose writing skills were equal to those of his brother
Henry, the novelist. Further, some of his teachings anticipate
the later work of the logical empiricists and no doubt inspired
positivist and analyst alike, e.g., James' "truth" thesis. "Truth
happens to an idea. It *becomes* true, is *made* true by events.
Its verity *is* in fact an event, a process: the process *namely*

of its verifying itself, its veri-*fication*. Its validity is the process of its vali-*dation*."[52]

John Dewey (1850–1952) was without doubt the most influential pragmatist, mainly because of his pioneering efforts in the field of education and his leadership in the social and ethical development of American philosophy and political practice. And, while Dewey preferred to call himself an experimentalist (based on the process of inquiry) or an instrumentalist (based on the process of acting on hypotheses to achieve a desired consequence), he was no less a radical empiricist than James. Describing his beliefs, he wrote, ". . . the essence of pragmatic instrumentalism is to conceive of *both* knowledge and practice as means of making goods—excellencies of all kinds—secure in experienced existence."[53] And elsewhere he insists that "experimentation enters into the determination of every warranted proposition."[54] Thus, for Dewey, philosophy is more than an academic pursuit (a spectator event), it is a social activity in which the individual interacts with the environment to resolve conflict and to achieve the desired change. He described philosophy as "a method of locating and interpreting the more serious of the conflicts that occur in life and a method of projecting ways of dealing with them."[55]

One of Dewey's important contributions to empirical philosophy is his newer version of experience, which no longer is passive observation, but the active use of observation to accomplish the desired modification of one's environment and thus to solve one's problems. He explained his revision of the more classical empiricism in the following way: "The empirical tradition is committed to particularism. Connections and continuities are supposed to be foreign to experience, to be by-products of dubious validity. An experience that is an undergoing of an environment and a striving for its control in new directions is pregnant with connections."[56] Thus, for Dewey, knowledge is a dynamic activity, not simply a static judgment on matters of little consequence to the potential knower. Further, according to Dewey, inquiry arises out of and aims to resolve the need

implicit in a problematic situation. This is the first step. As
Dewey says elsewhere:

> A disciplined mind takes delight in the problematic. . . . The questiona-
> ble becomes an active questioning, a search. . . . The scientific attitude
> may almost be defined as that which is capable of enjoying the doubtful;
> scientific method is in one aspect, a technique for making productive
> use of doubt by converting it into operations of definite inquiry.[57]

The second step in Dewey's problem-solving method of
knowledge is accomplished as consciousness of one's problems
leads to thought, reasoning and then action. Face to face with
our problems we think of ways similar problems have been
solved. We develop our hypotheses for solving the problems,
and we put into action a set of operations to accomplish our
goals and the desired consequences. Dewey describes his
method of inquiry in his book, *Logic: The Theory of Inquiry*.
In this essay he describes the formulation and use of hypotheses
as crucial to any investigation. Dewey's account of how hypotheses are constructed makes clear their operational nature. A
proposed hypothesis is considered plausible only insofar as it
can suggest experiments which will disclose those conditions
which most forcefully either verify or falsify the hypothesis.

Indeed, for Dewey, inquiry in general is guided along in
terms of operational interests. Both ideas and facts within the
context of inquiry are regarded as operational. Thus, ideas
are primarily for directing further operations of observation;
they are guidelines or plans for discovering new facts, while
also unifying the presently known facts. Facts, according to
Dewey, are operational in a number of ways. Some already
observed facts serve to suggest new ideas which in turn may
promote the discovery of additional facts. Newly discovered
facts operate evidentially by the way they link up with previously known facts. They serve to confirm, falsify, or modify
the hypothesis which has guided the inquiry up to the point
of their disclosure. This constant revision of hypothesis is a

serial process in which ideas are constantly tested until a solution becomes more and more tenable on the basis of wide experimental factual evidence.[58] For Dewey, this is knowledge—acting to solve problems by the process of thought, reasoning and experimenting until the problems are resolved or removed. In other words, knowledge is successful inquiry.

Dewey's philosophy of religion, like that of his predecessor, David Hume, is opposed to the identification of the religious with the supernatural. Dewey prefers the use of the word "religious," which designates a quality of experience, rather than "religion," which is a most ambiguous word at best.[59] Dewey points out that "religious" denotes an attitude that may be taken toward any object, goal or ideal. Moreover, he explains that "understanding and knowledge also enter into a perspective that is religious in quality. Faith in the sense of a continual disclosing of truth through directed cooperative human endeavor is more religious in quality than is any faith in a completed revelation. . . . [It is] faith in intelligence becoming religious in quality. . . ."[60]

Dewey's naturalism generally holds that *all* explanation should be limited to human experience, e.g., values, personality, beauty, community and religion, and that such explanation should be based on his philosophic (scientific, he calls it) method of inquiry. In his book, *A Common Faith,* Dewey recommends replacing the idea of "God" as a transcendent and supernatural being with the idea of "God" as representing an ideal for human action. This ideal would comprise a unification of ideal values or ends. Since the validity of such ideas as justice, love and goodness are undeniably linked to our ideas of realities that we call truth, God as an ideal need not be encumbered with the various dogmas and doctrines about his supernatural being that so often make the religious attitude unattractive for the modern mind.[61] And while Dewey does not mitigate his criticism of supernaturalist religion, he does opt for maintaining the name "God," if it is used to designate the working union of the ideal and the actual, "fed by every experience, no matter what its material." He finds such a use helpful/ fitting to counter the negative force of "aggressive atheism" which he notes has something in common with traditional super- naturalism, in that both induce in man "a sense of isolation and . . . consequent despair or defiance. . . ."[62] On the other hand, Dewey sees in his own religious attitude a "common faith" and naturalistic humanism, a practice which precludes alienation and despair by generating brotherhood and hope.

We have seen that Dewey's form of radical empiricism was at the same time a criticism of classical empiricism and a recon- struction of the traditional notion of experience on which all empirical philosophy is based. For Dewey, human experience implies that man is essential to the process, an "agent-patient," to use Dewey's term, who interacts with his environment to change it and is affected in turn by the interaction. Both Dewey and James before him proposed "radical empiricism" as an antidote to what they perceived to be the artificiality of the concept of experience in earlier classical empiricism. The Amer- ican pragmatists' prescription is that empirical philosophy should be more radical and attend more precisely to lived expe- rience and the real facts of a situation, discovered in experiment, inquiry and action. In this effort, both James and Dewey (in the spirit of Peirce) moved American philosophy closer to Euro- pean and British logical empiricism.[63]

2. Logical Empiricism—Hume's heirs in Europe

a. The Forerunners of Analytic Philosophy in England: Moore and Russell

George Edward Moore (1873–1958) is considered the father of the modern movement commonly called analytic philosophy. He recommended a "common sense" analysis of language, by which he meant a clarification of ordinary language to fit the criterion of common sense. Thus philosophy deals with those things, as Moore put it, ". . . which we all commonly assume to be true about the Universe, and which we are sure that we know to be true about it. . . ."[64] Further, in another book, *Principia Ethica*, Moore proclaimed an early version of analytic philosophy. In the preface to this essay he proposes that many of the most glaring controversies and perplexities that have characterized the history of philosophy would disappear if only thinkers would make quite clear precisely the nature of the questions which were raised. This would demand some perhaps initially difficult analysis and drawing of distinctions, but, urges Moore, this should be the program of a philosophical method that aims to be genuinely fruitful in solving all too perennial philosophical controversies.[65]

Still, in spite of Moore's prescience of the importance of the analysis of statements for meaning and reliability, he nevertheless implies a metaphysical view of reality to which he never gave his full attention. Because of this, Moore devoted little time to religion, electing the role of an agnostic to match his rejection of philosophic idealism.

Bertrand Russell (1872–1970) quite early in his career committed himself to the logical analysis of language. His goal was the replacement of defective symbols and the translation of misleading symbols into their correct logical form by means of the invention of a new language which would correspond exactly to the facts. Russell's "logical atomism" prescribed the use of words with clear, unambiguous meanings grounded in "sense-data." Such words were to be the "atoms" from which "atomic" or "molecular" propositions could be constructed—an ideal language in which both words and propositions would correspond to facts. Russell's essay, *Our Knowledge of the External World*, puts him firmly in the tradition of Hume and Mill. Given Russell's intellectual kinship to Mill, it is appropriate that Mill, in fact, was Russell's godfather.

However, it was Russell's book, *The Problems of Philosophy*, which firmly established him as a radical empiricist. It is an important book which reflects his quest for certainty and a further identification with empiricism. In it Russell acknowledges three different sorts of individual things in the world: "minds," "objects," and "sensed data" (Locke's "simple ideas of sense" or Hume's "impressions"). He also develops further his doctrine of knowledge by acquaintance which he first proposed in a paper in the *Proceedings of the Aristotelian Society.* He wrote: "We shall say that we have *acquaintance* with anything of which we are directly aware, without the intermediary process of inference or any knowledge of truths. Thus in the presence of my table I am acquainted with the sense data that make up the appearance of my table. . . ."[66] Further, while Russell holds that acquaintance is not "knowledge of *truths,*" but "knowledge of *things,*" he insists that "All our knowledge, both knowledge of things and knowledge of truths, rests upon acquaintance as its foundation."[67] Yet Russell in the true empirical spirit asks, "Granted that we are certain of our own sense-data, have we any reason for regarding them as signs of the existence of something else, which we can call the physical object?"[68]

Russell expressed his commitment to the program of analytic philosophy in an article titled "Logical Atomism." He states in this essay that the business of philosophy is logical analysis. While philosophy may be bold in proposing hypotheses which "science is not in a position to confirm or confute," its most important task is to criticize and clarify notions which are often assumed and are apt to be, as a result, unclear. Examples of such notions are mind, matter, consciousness, knowledge, experience, causality, will and time. Russell points out that all too often even the natural sciences are not as exact as they might be when such concepts as the aforementioned ones are uncritically and unclearly employed.[69] Russell's agnosticism and atheistic views are well known.[70] As late as 1957, Russell wrote in a preface to a re-publication of "Why I Am Not a Christian" and other essays on religion, "There has been a rumor in recent years to the effect that I have become less opposed to religious orthodoxy than I formerly was. This rumor is totally without foundation. I think all the great religions of the world—Buddhism, Hinduism, Christianity, Islam, and Communism—both untrue and harmful."[71]

The influence of Russell in the movement called analytic philosophy is beyond calculation. His contribution was important both in the import and genius of his own work as a logician and an empirical philosopher and as the instructor and tutor at Cambridge of many important philosophers, including Ludwig Wittgenstein. In the opinion of many historians of philosophy, Russell was the greatest philosopher of the twentieth century. There is little doubt that he was the best known.

3. Continental logical positivism—The Vienna Circle and Wittgenstein

The heirs of Hume on the European Continent are acknowledged to be the Vienna Circle, a group of scientists, mathematicians and philosophers who had gathered around Moritz Schlick, Professor of Philosophy at the University of Vienna. Other members were Rudolph Carnap, Herbert Feigl, Hans Hahn, Friedrich Waismann, Phillipp Frank (a physicist), Kurt Gödel (a mathematician), and Otto Neurath (a sociologist). In addition, other thinkers drifted in and out of the circle. Beyond the obvious influence of the empirical philosophy of Hume and Mill was the direct influence of Ernst Mach (1838–1916), a physicist and philosopher who was Schlick's predecessor at Vienna; the more indirect influences of Henri Poincaré and Albert Einstein and their views on scientific method; as well as the contributions to mathematical logic of Giuseppe Peano, Gottlieb Frege, Alfred North Whitehead and Russell.

But the greatest single influence on the Vienna Circle and the development of logical positivism was Ludwig Wittgenstein (1889–1951), a resident of Vienna and a pupil of Russell at Cambridge. As it happened, Wittgenstein's book, *Tractatus Logico—Philosophicus* (1919), became the "bible" of the Vienna Circle. In the book Wittgenstein had proclaimed the thesis of their movement: "The object of philosophy is the logical clarification of thoughts. Philosophy is not a theory but an activity. A philosophical work consists essentially of elucidations. The result of philosophy is not a number of 'philosophical propositions,' but to make propositions clear."[72] Yet the clarity of this passage cannot be said to be an example of the entire book. The *Tractatus* is a difficult book whose theses are more obvious than the meanings. Wittgenstein's main theses are: (1) that philosophical difficulties are the results of logical and linguistic misunderstandings; (2) that an ideal language isomorphic with reality is needed; (3) that propositions not isomorphic with reality are tautologies; and (4) that "whatever can be said at all can be said clearly," a theme which concluded with the warning, "Whereof one cannot speak [clearly], thereof one must be silent."[73]

The Vienna Circle published a "manifesto" in 1929, *Its Scientific World Outlook*, a pamphlet written chiefly by Carnap, Neurath and Hahn giving the aims and methods of the circle and demonstrating their thesis of the unification of the sciences through logical analysis, negatively removing metaphysical statements from meaningful knowledge, and positively clarifying the concepts and methods of the sciences to show that all knowledge is constructed from sense data. The other interrelated doctrines of the circle and logical positivism are: (1) the verifiability theory of meaning; (2) the traditional meaning and interpretation of logic and mathematics; (3) the legitimate business of philosophy as logical analysis; (4) the emotive theory of ethics; and (5) a conception of language as calculus.

The Vienna Circle's rejection of metaphysics is expressed quite clearly in this 1929 manifesto. According to the authors of the manifesto all statements such as "There is a God," "The first cause of the world is the Unconscious," or "There is an entelechy which is the leading principle in living things," are meaningless in so far as such statements allege to be descriptive of the nature of things. If they have any significance at all, it is only as an expression of the emotional attitude of the one who utters such statements. Since these statements

can neither be verified nor falsified the way claims in the empirical sciences can be, it is best to regard such claims, when
couched in the guise of metaphysical theory, as bad poetry
at best.[74]

The principle of verifiability adopted by the Vienna Circle
was derived mainly from Wittgenstein who had written in answer to the question, "How would one verify such an assertion?" ". . . to understand a proposition means to know what
is the case, if it is true,"[75] an answer which assumes empirical
verification. Based on this assumption, Schlick insisted that
"The meaning of a proposition is the method of its verification."
He argued:

> In order to understand a proposition we must be able exactly to indicate
> those particular circumstances that would make it true and those particu-
> lar circumstances that would make it false. "Circumstances" means facts
> of experience; and so experience decides the truth and falsity of proposi-
> tions, experience verifies. . . .[76]

Unfortunately, the Vienna Circle came to a premature end
in the early 1930s. The dissolution was begun by Schlick's
tragic and untimely murder and was completed by Nazi persecu-
tion of the surviving members of the group, as well as the
suppression of their publications in the middle of the decade.
Fortunately, the same decade also saw the rise of the most
influential logical positivist in the English-speaking world,
Alfred J. Ayer. Ayer spent some time with the members of
the Vienna Circle in 1932–33 following his studies at Oxford.
Then at age 25, in 1936, Ayer published *Language, Truth
and Logic*, a clever and abrasive book called by some "the
classic position of logical positivism." Indeed, at a conference
at the University of Delaware in the fall of 1979, Ayer admitted
that he is still a logical positivist, and perhaps the only one
remaining.

Ayer acknowledges his debt to the Vienna Circle, to Russell
and Wittgenstein, and ultimately to the empiricism of Berkeley

and Hume. As a faithful disciple of Hume, Ayer divided all genuine propositions into two classes; the relations of ideas, and matters of fact. He notes that the propositions concerning relations of ideas are the a priori propositions of logic and pure mathematics. These propositions, points out Ayer, are always certain and necessarily valid simply because they are analytic. As such, these propositions do not make any assertions about the empirical world, but "simply record our determination to use symbols in a certain fashion." On the other hand, propositions concerning empirical matters of fact can never be certain, but only probable. And, according to Ayer, the account of their method of validation also serves to explain the nature of truth. Continuing in the tradition of the Vienna Circle, Ayer adopts the empirical verification principle, albeit a "modified" one, to test whether a sentence expresses a genuine empirical hypothesis. The modified version of the verification principle requires only that "some possible sense-experience should be relevant to the determination of its truth or falsehood." According to Ayer, any statement which fails to satisfy this criterion is metaphysical and, as such, is neither true nor false but literally senseless. Ayer warns his readers that all too much of what currently passes for philosophical is metaphysical according to this criterion. Thus, for example, those philosophers who assert the existence of an immortal soul, a nonempirical world of values, or a transcendent God are speaking the nonsense of metaphysics.[77]

Ayer presents a well-argued case for the "elimination of metaphysics," criticizing what he calls a metaphysical pseudo-proposition of F. H. Bradley, ". . . the Absolute enters into, but is itself incapable of, evolution and progress," as "not even in principle verifiable."[78] Further, Ayer gives a "critique of ethics and theology," arguing that ". . . it is impossible to find a criterion for determining the validity of ethical judgments . . . they are pure expressions of feeling."[79] On the subject of theological utterances he wrote that ". . . to say that 'God exists' is to make a metaphysical utterance which cannot be either true or false. And . . . no sentence which purports to describe the nature of a transcendent god can possess any literal significance."[80] This position has amounted to what has been called "the positivist's veto" in the literature of philosophy and religion.

Completely loyal to the doctrines of the Vienna Circle, Ayer adopted a "weak" sense of the criterion of verifiability. In comparison to the "strong" sense of truth "conclusively established in experience," the "weak" sense asks "if it is possible for experience to render it possible,"[81] which Ayer admits in his revised introduction ten years later is "the only sense in which any proposition could conceivably be verified."[82]

4. British linguistic analysis—the "new" Wittgenstein, Ryle and others

A new point of view developed within the movement of analytic philosophy with the publication by Wittgenstein of *Philosophical Investigations* in 1953, which repudiated much of the *Tractatus* and more specifically his own "picture theory" of meaning in which a word names the reality it represents, and his insistence on the creation and use of an ideal language. Rather, he turned to the analysis of ordinary language and its diverse functions to eliminate what he called "philosophical puzzlement" (e.g., the problems encouraged by Platonism and Cartesianism). His most famous slogan, "the meaning is the use," brought new freshness and vigor to logical empiricism and made a consideration of metaphysics, ethics and religion possible. As he put it, "For a large class of cases—though not for all—in which we employ the term 'meaning' it can be defined thus: the meaning of a word is its use in the language."[83]

It is in the light of this new definition of meaning that many of the old philosophical puzzlements dissolve, according to Wittgenstein. Just as there are widely different sets of rules prescribing how the ball is played in basketball, tennis, football, or golf, each game thus with its own uniquely defined manner of ball play; so, too, different linguistic communities, differentiated by their varying forms of life or by different tasks, may employ what appear to be the same terms quite differently. This is what Wittgenstein has in mind when he speaks of "language games." Given that the meaning of a term employed in different contexts or language games may vary widely, it is all too common a mistake, according to Wittgenstein, to insist that there is some one Platonic-like "true" of the term.

Wittgenstein suggests that philosophical investigation can profit from attention to ordinary language—to its context, use and language games. When philosophers ask, "what are these words to be used for now? the language game in which they are to be applied is missing."[84] Whenever perplexed by the meaning of a concept, let us say the concept of "good," Wittgenstein prescribes: "In such a difficulty always ask yourself: How did we *learn* the meaning of this word ('good' for instance)? From what sort of examples? in what language games? Then it will be easier for you to see that the word must have a family of meanings."[85] Wittgenstein's concern for language therapy thus ruled out the positivist's veto. "To say: 'This combination of words makes no sense' excludes it from the sphere of language and thereby bounds the domain of language . . . . When a sentence is called senseless, it is not as it were its sense that is senseless. But a combination of words is being excluded from the language, withdrawn from circulation."[86]

Gilbert Ryle, sometime tutor of Ayer, early gave expression to the method of analytic philosophy in his paper, "Systematically Misleading Expressions," published in *Proceedings of the Aristotelian Society*, 1931–32. In this paper, Ryle proposes that the "sole and whole function of philosophy" consists of the clarification of expressions in which the real form of the fact recorded is somehow obscured or disguised. Ryle calls this task "philosophical analysis." When philosophical analysis is properly executed, it succeeds in stating in a new form of words the fact which others failed to exhibit.[87] Ryle, an early follower of Moore, Russell and Wittgenstein, sought the elimination of conceptual confusions in philosophy which result from the acceptance of grammatical for logical similarities and difference. In so doing, he developed analytic techniques which brought him quite close to the "new" Wittgenstein. Ryle's *The Concept of Mind* (1949) is evidence of the influence of Wittgenstein on his thought. In it Ryle developed a clever analysis of what he called "the Ghost in the Machine," in which he attacked Descartes' particular form of dualism in which the mind or soul was a "ghost" in a material body. For Ryle, Cartesianism is a "category mistake." The mistake consists of "representing the facts of a concept as if they belonged to one logical type or category when they actually belong to another."[88] The mechanics of category mistake is well illustrated in my book, *Language and Concepts in Christian Education.* Herein I define it as "the use of a word in the wrong logical category, [e.g.] confusing explanation and description with evaluation and prescription."[89]

While *The Concept of Mind* is a helpful and significant example of the use of linguistic analysis to clarify the puzzlements of traditional philosophy, Ryle's book *Dilemmas* is even more helpful in exhibiting the application of analytical philosophy to the several domains of concern, including philosophical theology. He defines dilemmas as "wrongly imputed parities of reasoning." Some dilemmas in philosophy arise from the differences in viewpoints and methodologies. While Ryle was not personally interested in theological language and explanation, his agreement with Wittgenstein on the rules of language games and the wider view of meaning this involves, based on context, use and language games, gives some encouragement to philosophers of religion.

His account of category mistakes provides a useful standpoint from which controversies in the philosophy of religion, which appear to be unresolvable, may be resolved. When thinkers believe that they contradict one another, their disagreement, Ryle points out, often turns out to be merely verbal. In some

cases such an apparent disagreement often disappears when
the thinkers can be shown that what they take to be rival
answers to the same question are really answers to two different
questions. This talking at cross purposes, according to Ryle,
is often something that can be clearly exhibited by showing
how each of the disputants, at certain points, base their arguments upon concepts of different categories. It is the task of
linguistic analysis to show in detail to what degree both sides
employ concepts which are either more or less commensurate
than the contestants had supposed.[90]

Of course it is not only in philosophy of religion that analytical philosophy's demand for precision, and its elucidation of
fundamental concepts, has played an influential and important
role. Numerous analytic essays in areas such as ethics, law,
philosophy of science, and sociology have been published and
gained a wide reading.[91] The seminal work of such analytic
thinkers as G. E. Moore, Wittgenstein, Ayer and Ryle is carried
forward by heirs who have applied their techniques to an ever-
widening domain of disciplines.

Ian T. Ramsey noted, in his article "Contemporary Empiricism," that the development of empiricism in recent years "has
concentrated on the problem of meaning [which] has turned
our attention to the contextual setting of words and the patterns
of behaviour into which words and sentences are interlocked.
If at this stage we wish to formulate any interim conclusions
which might have bearing on philosophical theology, we might
list them as three:

(1) Let us not look for 'objects' as the meaning of words. Nor would
this slogan exclude such words as 'God' or 'the soul.'
(2) When presented with problematical words, look always at the discourse and behaviour in which such words are set.
(3) In particular, let us be alert to the empirical grounding of this
discourse.[92]

And A. G. N. Flew's new slogan from Hume for *Logic and
Language II* reflects the newer and more comprehensive role
for philosophy; no less analytical and critical, but broader and

more comprehensive, reflecting the "new" Wittgenstein, Ryle and others.

> And though a philosopher may live remote from business, the genius of philosophy, if carefully cultivated by several, must gradually diffuse itself throughout the whole society and bestow a similar correctness on every art or calling.[93]

D. A Summary and a Look Ahead

Our all-too-brief review of empirical philosophy, ending as it has with a reminder of the traditional comprehensiveness of philosophy at its best, has revealed some aberrations of a broader understanding of empiricism. For instance, the skepticism of Hume in the name of epistemology, the situational utilitarianism of pragmatism in the name of truth, and the positivist veto of metaphysics, ethics and religion in the name of meaning speak to a much more limited view and practice of the "genius of philosophy." Fortunately we have been able to notice redeeming movements within the various manifestations of empirical philosophy. These movements have strained against and finally overcome the limitations imposed on the doing of philosophy by the more extreme empiricists, namely Hume and Ayer, and opened the horizons and the matching expressions and explanations to the consideration of "every art or calling."

In the next chapter we will concern ourselves with a consideration of the result of the philosophical analyses of theological language under the title, "Empirical Theology." We will survey several fruitful sources of this unusual area of theology: first, the British philosophical analysts who turned their attention to religious language, John Wisdom, Antony Flew, Richard Hare, Basil Mitchell, R. B. Braithwaite, Ian Crombie and Alasdair MacIntyre; second, the American naturalists and phenomonologists H. N. Wieman and J. H. Randall, Jr.; and third, the American philosophical analysts who also concerned themselves with empirical theology. We will carefully examine their analyses and assess their contributions and successes as a preparation for the consideration of the Christian empiricism of Ian Ramsey.

III. EMPIRICAL THEOLOGY:
The Philosophical Analyses of Theological Language

A. Introduction

For many, the title "Empirical Theology"might well suggest a contradiction in terms or a misleading concept. We have noted that historically the word "empirical" describes knowledge based on experience or having reference to actual facts obtained from the observation of the senses. And we are aware that the word "theology," which means literally "the study of God," describes an epistemological procedure which is generally described as nonempirical. Nevertheless, a theology which claims that its fundamental propositions are indeed based on experience, or are accepted because they are necessary generalizations from experience, may qualify to be called "empirical." Such usage often denies some of the usual philosophical foundations of traditional theology, such as special revelations, innate or a priori concepts and the necessity of reason to support their tenets. Indeed, some of the practitioners of empirical theology have generally opposed dogmatic theology in favor of reference to religious experience which could be verified by ordinary scientific or language procedures. Friedrich Schleiermacher and Rudolf Otto are examples of such practitioners. In this chapter we will examine the contribution of a number of contemporary philosophers and theologians to a growing interest in empirical theology, considering the analyses of both British and American analytic philosophers and two American naturalists.

B. British Philosophical Analyses of Theological Language

"Perhaps if ideas and words were distinctly weighed and duly considered, they would afford us another sort of logic and critic than what we have hitherto been acquainted with."[1] These words of John Locke, which begin A. G. N. Flew's Introduction to *Essays in Logic and Language* (First Series),[2] link classical and contemporary empiricism with the movement of analytic philosophy which currently prevails among the philosophical faculties of Oxford, Cambridge and London and also expects a strong influence elsewhere in the United Kingdom, Australia and the United States.

One of Flew's criteria for the selection of articles was that they could be read and readily understood by the layman who was untutored in the terminology of academic philosophy. This, Flew says, causes them to "stand squarely in the British tradition of . . . John Locke, of Bishop Berkeley and David Hume. It was Berkeley who proclaimed in the first draft of the Introduction to his *Principles of Human Knowledge* that 'I shall throughout endeavor to express myself in the clearest, plainest and most familiar manner, abstaining from all hard and unusual terms which are pretended by those that use them to cover a sense abstracted and sublime.' "[3] Further, the collection was to include articles in as many as possible of the major branches of philosophy including ethics, political philosophy and the philosophy of religion. And, while disowning any party labels, e.g., logical positivism, etc., still the unifying theme of the book was indicated by Wittgenstein's and Ryle's programatic definitions of philosophy: "All philosophy is 'Critique of language,' " (Wittgenstein) and philosophy is at least "the detection of the sources in linguistic idioms of recurrent misconstructions and absurd theories."[4] (Ryle)

The application of analytic techniques to the problems of religious language was represented by John Wisdom, pupil and successor at Cambridge of Wittgenstein, whose article "Gods" revealed the mistake of accepting grammatical similarity for logical similarity in the case of the "invisible and intangible gardener" of his clever and now famous parable. Wisdom begins his paper by noting that "the existence of God is not an experimental issue in the way that it was" and that Elijah's experiment on Mount Carmel to prove that Yahweh is the *true* (and existent) God "Would be far less appropriate today. . . ." Further, he notes that "belief in gods is not merely a matter of expectation of a world to come,"[5] although many theists believe just that.

Wisdom then asks how are theists and atheists to be differentiated. Surely, Wisdom suggests, it cannot be as simple as claiming something like "theists are superstitious" or "atheists are blind." On the contrary, according to Wisdom, there are various sources from within the many-sided experiences of life that may provide credible rationales for belief in the divine.[6] Indeed, he comments, when we examine the logic of belief (accepting the reasonableness of belief in human minds), we immediately find at least two sources: one metaphysical, the other scientific, prompting such questions as, Are there divine minds? and Are there facts in nature to support our beliefs in divine minds? But Wisdom shows there is also a personal source for the statements, "I believe in God," and "I do not." Wisdom asks, "Is this merely the putting of a name?" and "What's in a name?" And he answers both "nothing" and "very much," since facts give different answers to such questions.

Wisdom suggests that the statement, " 'There is a God' evinces an attitude to the familiar" as a persuasion which may "start by being experimental and gradually become something quite different. . . ." At this point he presents his now famous parable of the gardener.

Two people return to their long neglected garden and find among the weeds a few of the old plants surprisingly vigourous. One says to the other, "It must be that a gardener has been coming and doing something about these plants." Upon inquiry they find that no neighbour has ever seen anyone at work in their garden. The first man says to the other, "He must have worked while people slept." The other says, "No, someone would have heard him and besides, anybody who cared about the plants would have kept down these weeds." The first man says, "Look at the way these are arranged. There is purpose and a feeling for beauty here. I believe that someone comes, someone invisible to mortal eyes. I believe that the more carefully we look the more we shall find confirmation of this." They examine the garden ever so carefully and sometimes they come on new things suggesting that a gardener comes and sometimes they come on new things suggesting the contrary and even that a malicious person has been at work. Besides examining the garden carefully they also study what happens to gardens left without attention. Each learns all the other learns about this and about the garden. Consequently, when after all this, one says, "I still believe a gardener comes" while the other says, "I don't" their different words now reflect no difference as to what they have found in the garden, no difference as to what they would find in the garden if they looked further and no difference about how fast untended gardens fall into disorder. At this stage, in this context, the gardener hypothesis has ceased to be experimental, the difference between one who accepts and one who rejects it is now not a matter of the one expecting something the other does not expect. What is the difference between them? The one says, "A gardener comes unseen and unheard. He is manifested only in his works with which we are all familiar." The other says, "There is no gardener" and with this difference in what they say about the gardener goes a difference in how they feel towards the garden, in spite of the fact that neither expects anything of it which the other does not expect.[7]

Wisdom goes on to note that the theist and the atheist do not disagree about the empirical facts (the experimental and the observational). The disagreement is now a question of naming, "There is," or "There isn't" which is not an empirical but a metaphysical judgment and dependent on attitudes and feelings. However, theists do speak of trans-sensual and trans-scientific facts. Is there any way to settle this issue?

Wisdom asks whether there is any kind of logic which underlies the expression of an attitude in the utterance of a word, or in the application of a name such as "Lord" or "Heavenly Father." He answers that we cannot settle the theistic issue by logical calculation, by deduction from the facts we know (as Aquinas tried). Wisdom suggests there might be some help from the methods of the courts of law, where judgments are made in an accumulative (horizontal) process, including facts and attitudes which account for the decision. Thus, Wisdom concludes there is no right or wrong about the existence of God. It is not experimental (no facts, absolute rationality) but consists only in feelings and attitudes. And he recommends a "connecting technique" similar to that "used in revealing . . . beauty, in removing blindness, in inducing an attitude which is lacking, in reducing a reaction that is inappropriate."[8] Wisdom mentions "connections" in aesthetics, in which we relook, reexamine to "see" form and relation, and then points out some necessary "disconnections" such as vagueness and ambiguity and "unspoken connections," or "connections we had missed" (the excellence of Picasso).

Wisdom not only asks what constitutes the rationale for belief in God, but he also asks what is it that happens in us when we inquire into the grounds of belief in God. We can only understand these grounds, points out Wisdom, when we are able to relive or identify with those feelings which are expressed or objectified in religious belief. Thus, to understand Wordsworth's notion of the Divine in "Tintern Abbey," we must be able to feel with Wordsworth that "the world is haunted, that something watches in the hills and manages the stars."[9] In short, feelings prevail both in the original expressions of belief in God and in any subsequent appreciation of the grounds of these beliefs. So, too, stories of the gods and the analogies of parents and grandparents to the deities provoke feelings, but they can be taken in different ways, as by theists and atheists—or by theologians and psychologists like Sigmund Freud, who hold different attitudes and opinions on religion and propose different ways of salvation.

As for Wisdom himself, he expresses appreciation for the constructive role religious claims play in elevating human life. He points out that many have searched for salvation and the reports they bring back whether in words, music, or paint are always incomplete and thus may mislead others. Nevertheless, their statements are not useless and those ones which speak of our unity with God may be very edifying. Thus, Wisdom regards St. John's teaching, that God is in us as we love one another, as an example of a useful doctrine.[10]

Elsewhere, Wisdom has developed a theory of "linguistic penetration"[11] to deal with paradoxes and expressions of attitudes and feelings. He recommends that we take such statements seriously and avoid the positivist's veto. According to Wisdom, we often do not properly apprehend the nature of a paradox until we have become explicitly aware of the contradictions with which it confronts our reason, and yet at the same time find it a practical necessity to go on living with the unresolved contradictions. It is only when this tension, repeated a number of times in our intellectual life, gives way to a state of mind where we are no longer driven to assert or deny the paradox, that we have come to appreciate the intractable character of what is really a paradox. Wisdom's article "Gods" accepts the oddness of what appears to be linguistic confusions and by linguistic penetration of the more informal logics of language usage moves beyond the facts to notice the significance of attitudes and feelings toward patterns of life which otherwise we would or could not notice.

Wisdom's article "Gods" also provided a critical rejoinder to a new discussion between philosophers and theologians wherein the techniques of analytic philosophy were applied to theological issues. The collection of twenty-two essays and papers, *New Essays in Philosophical Theology*, edited by A. G. N. Flew and A. MacIntyre[12] typified this discussion.

The essay, "Theology and Falsification," first published as a discussion (1950–1951) in the British periodical *University*, is an especially good example of the analytic approach to theological questions.

Antony G. N. Flew, editor of the two series, *Essays on Logic and Language*, and co-editor of *New Essays*, opened the debate with a short, provocative paper in the empiricist-positivist mode which speaks to the main problem he sees in meaningful theological language—not simply its unverifiability, but its unfalsifiability. The latter suggests that for a statement to be cognitively meaningful it must have a conceivable empirical event which could show it to be false. To illustrate his claim, Flew reconstructs Wisdom's parable.

Once upon a time two explorers came upon a clearing in the jungle. In the clearing were growing many flowers and many weeds. One explorer says, "Some gardener must tend this plot." The other disagrees, "There is no gardener." So they pitch their tents and set a watch. No gardener is ever seen. "But perhaps he is an invisible gardener." So they set up a barbed-wire fence. They electrify it. They patrol with bloodhounds. (For they remember how H. G. Wells's *The Invisible Man* could be both smelt and touched though he could not be seen.) But no shrieks ever suggest that some intruder has received a shock. No movements of the wire ever betray an invisible climber. The bloodhounds never give cry. Yet still the Believer is not convinced. "But there is a gardener, invisible, intangible, insensible to electric shocks, a gardener who has no scent and makes no sound, a gardener who comes secretly to look after the garden which he loves." At last the Sceptic despairs, "But what remains of your original assertion? Just how does what you call an invisible, intangible, eternally elusive gardener differ from an imaginary gardener or even from no gardener at all?"[13]

Flew then notes that while the parable "starts as an assertion, that something exists or that there is some analogy between certain complexes of phenomena," it may be reduced to an expression of a "picture preference" (A Wisdom notion). As Flew points out, "A fine brash hypothesis may thus be killed by inches, the death by a thousand qualifications."[14] This is the main problem with theological utterances, they look like ordinary assertions, that such and such is the case (or its equivalent, such and such is not the case), yet in the case of theological statements, it is not at all clear what would really count against their truth. Flew concludes with a challenge. He asks what would have to occur in order to constitute a disproof of God's existence or the claim that God, like a heavenly Father, loves us. We see a child dying of inoperable cancer of the throat and his frantic earthly father desperately trying to help, but see no clear sign of his heavenly Father's concern. Perhaps the believer is able yet to rescue his belief with some kind of qualification. Thus he tells himself that God's love is "not a merely human love" or that it is "an inscrutable love." Perhaps the believer is reassured. But we might ask what is this assurance of God's love, qualified in this way, worth? What, asks Flew, would have to happen not merely (morally and wrongly) to tempt but also (logically and rightly) to lead us to repudiate our claim that there is a loving God?[15]

Flew's contribution to the ongoing dialogue of philosophical theology can well be assessed at the point of this estimable challenge to theology and to the intelligibility of theological explanation. As a vocal agnostic he was a helpful and persistent catalyst in the post World War II discussions in the philosophy of religion. And he continues to be such a force, for instance, in his 1976 debate with Thomas B. Warren at North Texas State University on the existence of God.

Richard M. Hare, a widely respected Oxford analyst, offers a response to Flew's challenge, defending religion, not Christianity per se, as a prior consideration. He acknowledges the unassailable position of logical empiricism and admits elsewhere that theologians have not explained convincingly the use of religious language. In this respect, Hare suggests, theologians are like those gardeners who cannot tell us either correctly or clearly how they cultivate their plants so well.[16] Hare shifts the ground by relating another parable.

A certain lunatic is convinced that all dons want to murder him. His friends introduce him to all the mildest and most respectable dons that they can find, and after each of them has retired, they say, "You see, he doesn't really want to murder you; he spoke to you in a most cordial manner; surely you are convinced now?" But the lunatic replies, "Yes, but that was only his diabolical cunning; he's really plotting against me the whole time, like the rest of them; I know it I tell you." However many kindly dons are produced, the reaction is still the same.[17]

Hare now applies Flew's test to his hero and decides that nothing will count against his belief. Indeed, such a belief is both unverifiable and unfalsifiable and asserts nothing. Yet it does express both a conviction and an interpretation of one's experience. Hare calls such a belief (or several related beliefs) a "blik," a term which he never completely defines. However, we do know that it is not an assertion and nothing can falsify it. A "blik" is therefore nonlogical and immune to contrary argument, yet it is the basis for, as Hume taught us, "our whole commerce with the world . . . [and] without a *blik* there can be no explanation; for it is by our *bliks* that we decide what is and what is not an explanation."[18]

Hare's reference to Hume at this point is important, for Hare's "bliks," or as Hume calls them "natural beliefs," are not observations but attitudes and thus do not affect the empirical decision directly. However, they are indirectly effective, providing a framework for beliefs "we embrace by a kind of instinct or natural impulse on account of their suitability and conformity to the mind."[19] Hume points out in his *Treatise* that all knowledge is attended by imperfections, e.g., the perception of constant conjunction, from which we infer objects. He contends that such imperfections extend to religion since religious beliefs are not matters of fact nor grounded upon relation of ideas (logic). Thus, for Hume, religious beliefs, while not falsifiable assertions, are nonetheless "sensitive beliefs," acquired with the force of a sensation and available to reason and therefore escape the skepticism inevitable under the canons of verifiability and falsifiability which must be applied to all straightforward assertions.

Hare calls Flew mistaken for regarding religious language as though it provided explanations in the same way scientists regard explanations. But for Hare religious language (a system of "bliks") has a content which evinces an attitude (or attitudes) which make an important difference in the daily life of the believer. As Hare points out in "Religion and Morals," ". . . there is no distinction between fact and illusion for a person who does not take up a certain attitude to the world."[20] Hare finally chides Flew on his version of Wisdom's parable, arguing that "the explorers do not *mind* about their garden," whereas "It is because I mind very much about what goes on in the garden in which I find myself, that I am unable to share the explorers' detachment."[21] In sum, Hare accepts the limitations logical empiricism imposes upon religious language, but offers a functional, not a cognitive usage to overcome its veto.

In the long view, however, Hare does not succeed in answering Flew's challenge. For the religious orthodox, Hare's theory of "bliks" emasculates the content of religious assertions beyond the point of even minimum objectivity. And for those seeking an understanding and explanation of religious attitudes, Hare's need to distinguish between right and wrong "bliks" moves the judgment on religious beliefs to a new field of human concern just as difficult as the field of religious language—the language of valuation.

Basil Mitchell, who later was to become Ramsey's successor to the chair of Nolloth Professor of the Philosophy of the Christian Religion at Oxford, presented a response both to Flew's original challenge and to Hare's revisionary effort. Mitchell notes that Flew conducts the theologian's case oddly. According to Mitchell, Flew has mistakenly minimized the way in which theologians do take into account facts which may count against religious belief. After all, points out Mitchell, theologians deal with such intractable problems as the problem of evil just because they take seriously such facts as the suffering of children. It is true that the believing theologian will not allow anything to decisively falsify his faith in God's goodness. The believer, after all, notes Mitchell, is not a detached observer, but is committed to God.

To illustrate his point of view, Mitchell offers another parable

which he suggests is closer to the situation from which claims
to know in religion arise:

> Perhaps this can be brought out by yet another parable. In time of
> war in an occupied country, a member of the resistance meets one night
> a stranger who deeply impresses him. They spend that night together
> in conversation. The Stranger tells the partisan that he himself is on
> the side of the resistance—indeed that he is in command of it, and
> urges the partisan to have faith in him no matter what happens. The
> partisan is utterly convinced at that meeting of the Stranger's sincerity
> and constancy and undertakes to trust him.
>
> They never meet in conditions of intimacy again. But sometimes the
> Stranger is seen helping members of the resistance, and the partisan
> is grateful and says to his friends, "He is on our side."
>
> Sometimes he is seen in the uniform of the police handing over
> patriots to the occupying power. On these occasions his friends murmur
> against him: but the partisan still says, "He is on our side." He still
> believes that, in spite of appearances, the Stranger did not deceive him.
> Sometimes he asks the Stranger for help and receives it. He is then
> thankful. Sometimes he asks and does not receive it. Then he says,
> "The Stranger knows best." Sometimes his friends, in exasperation,
> say, "Well, what *would* he have to do for you to admit that you were
> wrong and that he is not on our side?" But the partisan refuses to
> answer. He will not consent to put the Stranger to the test. And sometimes
> his friends complain, "Well, if *that's* what you mean by his being on
> our side, the sooner he goes over to the other side the better."[22]

Mitchell concludes from the parable that the partisan does
not allow anything to count decisively against his belief that
the Stranger is his ally because the partisan has committed
himself to trust the Stranger. However, the partisan's faith is
tested by the ambiguous behavior of the Stranger and in this
sense such behavior is recognized by the partisan as counting
against his belief in the Stranger.

Further, Mitchell points out that it is in this respect that
his parable differs from Hare's. The partisan is able to acknowledge that many facts may and do count against his belief.
Nothing, on the other hand, can count against the lunatic's
blik about dons which Hare describes. Moreover, the partisan's

initial commitment to the Stranger is founded upon the partisan's reasonable assessment of the Stranger's good character. Yet Mitchell agrees with Flew that theological utterances are assertions. And Mitchell wants to hold that religious belief is in some way an explanation that makes sense of human behavior in a situation which will vary in the interpretations of the facts involved. While Christian doctrines cannot be conclusively falsifiable, they should not then be regarded either as vacuous claims which have no connection with experience or as provisional hypotheses readily discarded when faith seems too strained by its present credal formulations. Rather, observes Mitchell, the committed Christian will continue to affirm them as significant articles of faith.[23]

William T. Blackstone has characterized Mitchell's response as "right-wing,"[24] and James A. Martin, Jr.[25] suggests that Mitchell moves the discussion in a personalist direction, a move most compatible with Ramsey's personalist position. Certainly, Mitchell's position will allow for the more traditional apologetics and theodices and provide for an interpretation of religious language which would preserve both its objectivity (one can believe in the object of our believable experiences) and the import of the believer's commitment. However, in the view of the philosopher, the conclusions of the believer may well be entirely subjective or share the fate of overly qualified hypotheses—meaninglessness.

In Flew's concluding remarks, which consist of replies to Mitchell and Hare, he restates the basic problem, i.e., that theological utterances are intended to provide explanations ("Why this particular thing occurs; *and not something else*") or express assertions ("claim that things stand thus and thus; *and not otherwise*").[26] If it is otherwise, explanations in religious language are bogus and assertions are vacuous. Flew praises Mitchell for his admirably honest and straightforward rejoinder to Flew's characterization of the theologian as a purveyor of unfalsifiable claims. Yet, Flew argues that Mitchell's parable does not explain God's love (the Stranger is a man with believable excuses) in the face of the presence of pain. Thus, points out Flew, since God is omnipotent we cannot say that he would like to help but he is unable. Nor can we say that he would help if only he knew; for God, unlike the Stranger, is omniscient. It also will not do to blame others for wickedness, since God creates these others. Indeed, logic requires that if we assert the omnipotence and omniscience of God, then God must be implicated in every moral defect of the universe. Ultimately, concludes Flew, God must be responsible for the evil that haunts the world. The logic here is inescapable and should Mitchell wish to blunt its force he could do so only by means of an increasingly strained series of qualifications. Such qualifications, warns Flew, multiplied apparently indefinitely, not only would violate normal canons of logic but also would inevitably constitute the failure of faith.[27] And in the end Flew says that Mitchell would have to switch to qualification and "death by a thousand qualifications . . . would . . . constitute 'a failure in faith as well as logic.' "

Flew labels Hare's contribution "fresh and bold" for his introduction of the concept of *blik* which would shift Christian religious utterances from assertions to expressions of a *blik* or an attitude. However, Flew challenges Hare on two counts. First, "if Hare's religion is a *blik,* involving no cosmological assertions about the nature and activities of a supposed personal creator," is he an orthodox Christian? Second, if theological utterances are "not even intended as assertions then many religious activities would become fraudulent, or merely silly."[28]

Flew concludes by warning philosophers of religion of the danger of "doublethink" as described by George Orwell in his novel *1984.* Doublethink, often committed by the ruling elite in Orwell's account of a negative utopia, consists of holding and believing two contradictory claims simultaneously. The party intellectual of Orwell's *1984* knows that he is playing tricks with reality, but through the exercise of doublethink he deludes himself that reality is not violated. Flew asks whether or not religious intellectuals are also driven to doublethink to maintain their belief in a loving God in the face of an often evil and indifferent world.

Richard B. Braithwaite's introduction to his Eddington Memorial Lecture, delivered at his Cambridge inaugural, "An Empiricist's View of the Nature of Religious Belief," sketches the development of the empiricist tradition and acknowledges the importance of the verification principle by quoting A. S. Eddington's article written in 1925: "The scientist and the religious teacher may well be content to agree that the value of any hypothesis extends just so far as it is verified by actual experience."[29] Braithwaite then compares religious statements with three classes of statements whose method of truth value testing is clear and unchallenged: (1) "statements about particular empirical facts . . . testable by direct observation," (2) "scientific hypotheses and other general empirical statements," and (3) "logically necessary statements of logic and mathematics (and their contradictories)."[30] He argues that religious statements fit into any of the three classes and notes that they have the same "peculiarity" as moral statements and therefore have meaning ascertained, as Wittgenstein suggested, by the way the statements are used. Yet Braithwaite still insists that the only way of discovering how a religious statement is used is by empirically investigating the manner in which its use expresses the conviction of the believer.

Braithwaite then claims that inquiry justifies his thesis that religious statements are used as, indeed, they are assimilated into, moral assertions and serve an ethical function. Thus his view of the use of religious statements is part of his wider "conative" theory of ethics. Braithwaite insists that moral assertions assert an intention to perform an action or declare a commitment to a way of life, and it is this intention that becomes the criterion for the meaningfulness of the assertion. Applying the conative theory to religious assertions, Braithwaite notes that they also express both intention and commitment. Hence the meaning of a religious assertion is to be identified with the way its use expresses the asserter's resolve to follow a specified policy of behavior. According to Braithwaite, the actual intention of the Christian to follow in Christ's pattern of living is not only the proof of the sincerity of his Christian beliefs, but this intention stands as the only criterion for the meaningfulness of his asserted beliefs. Further, Braithwaite comments on the Christian's assertion that God is love (the epitome of the Christian religion) and interprets this utterance as a declaration of intention to follow an "agapeistic way of life. " Indeed, he exclaims, "I myself take the typical meaning of the body of Christian assertions as being given by their proclaiming intentions to follow an agapeistic way of life,"[31] and gives 1 Corinthians 13 as an "empirical description" of such a commitment.

Braithwaite admits there are differences between religious and moral assertions; e.g., a religious behavior policy is composed of a set of assertions as compared to a single assertion, and moral teaching in religion is given by concrete examples as compared to the more abstract moral assertions. Further, religious behavioral patterns entail both an external and an internal change. But in accounting for differences between the religions, Braithwaite notes that in each religion the intention to pursue certain behavioral patterns is associated with a set of stories. It is these stories which form the context within which religious commitments to follow a particular faith are made. "To assert the whole set of assertions of the Christian religion," therefore, "is both to tell the Christian doctrinal story and to confess allegiance to the Christian way of life."[32] Indeed, Braithwaite spells out what he considers to be the necessary and sufficient conditions for the proper use of "Christian." A person is a professing Christian, according to Braithwaite, if he both professes to live following Christian moral principles and at the same time associates his conformity to these principles with the meaning of the Christian stories. It is not necessary, however, adds Braithwaite, to believe that the empirical propositions presented within the stories correspond to empirical matters of fact.

In summary, Braithwaite returns to a consideration of religious beliefs and follows the same line of reasoning as he did with assertions. Like moral beliefs, religious beliefs are not a species of beliefs in propositions, but are declarations of intention to behave in a certain way identified with certain stories associated with the believer's intention. In this way the believer's claim for meaningfulness can be taken seriously by the empiricist. Thus when religious statements are concerned with human behavior they are both cognitive and meaningful. To claim that "Jesus is the Son of God" is noncognitive and meaningless by itself, but as an announcement of a Christian's intention to follow Jesus as the stories about him suggest and engage in Christian-like behavior, the statement is meaningful.

Most of his peers agree that Braithwaite has offered a unique and challenging analysis of religious language. Yet like the analyses of both Flew and Hare, many religious traditionalists have rejected Braithwaite's conative theory of theological utterance. Further, even empathetic critics point out that there is some residue of vagueness and ambiguity in classifying all religious language as a kind of moral language, and also that there is little gained by the reduction to the contestable, preferential and prescriptive field of ethics.

Ian M. Crombie contributed a later paper, "Theology and Falsification," described by the editors of *New Essays* as "arising from the *University* Discussion," and another "right wing" response in answer to Flew's challenge and the several other responses. Crombie begins by dismissing statements like "God exists" since such statements asserting existence have their own logical difficulties. He then notes that while statements about God consist of the usual two parts, subject (that which is said) and predicate (that which it is said about), yet when the subject-word is "God" the predicate is composed of "ordinary words put to un-ordinary uses," i.e., "God loves us."

Crombie also makes a few observations about the epistemological nature of religious belief, noting that it has two parents (and a nurse). (1) The logical mother is *undifferentiated* theism,

the elements in our experience which lead to belief in, or attitude toward God, e.g., a sense of contingency, moral experience,
the beautiful and the mystical. Expressions of these elements
are at best quasi-arguments, not logical-scientific assertions and
thus do not possess literal meaning. (2) The logical father is
particular events or occasions as manifestations of the divine,
of which Crombie said, "in thinking of certain events in terms
of the category of the divine, we can give what seems to us
the most convincing account of them, that we can assure ourselves that the notion of God is not just an empty aspiration."[33]
(3) The nurse is the nurture provided by religious activity as
belief is nurtured by the practice of the Christian life.

However, Crombie insists that belief must be related to that
which is experienced as revelatory of God. This is why belief
must involve an element of authority. When the Christian
speaks about God, he speaks by virtue of the authority of
Christ. It is at this point that Crombie introduces his notion
of religious language as parable, which he uses in an extended
sense. For example, in the story of the Prodigal Son, we come
to understand the religious assertion "God loves us as a father"
as the loving human father runs to meet and forgive his penitent
son. But it, and others like it, is more than merely a story,
for in the parable we are referred, in faith, to the truth of
God otherwise beyond our comprehension. The parable, explains Crombie, points beyond itself. There is no literal resem-
blance between the truth to which it points and the features
of the story. For the believer the parable is accepted as providing a trustworthy reflection of the unfamiliar and transcendent
reality in terms of more familiar episodes of human experience.[34] It is the person of Christ himself that provides the
warranty for Crombie's parabolic method. Both in his acts and
teachings Christ is our authoritative parabler. And while
through parables it is as though we see in a glass darkly, we
can be confident that with Christ as their source we shall not
be misled. Believing the parables and interpreting them in
the light of one another, the Christian is confident that he

has the knowledge from which the foundation of the religious life is built.[35]

Crombie now returns to the basic question of the *University* discussion taking up the issue of the verification and falsification of religious claims. He concedes that something could count against the claim that God is loving and merciful, for example, suffering does. Crombie further concedes that suffering which was utterly, eternally and irredeemably pointless could decidedly falsify the claim about God's mercy.[36] But the believer holds to the truth of this claim. And since no crucial experiment can ever decisively inform us of the whole picture, which must remain beyond the reach of any possible experience, nothing ever will decisively count against the believer's assertion. Crombie concludes that with his explication he has assured the communication value of religious statements by developing a parabolic method. In this method falsifiability and verifiability are irrelevant; the best test for meaningful discourse is human experience of a divine encounter. Thus, for the Christian, Jesus Christ is both "the verification and to some extent also the specification, of the divine love, and further in the concrete realities of the Christian life" the divine love of God may be encountered.[37]

Truly Crombie has given a "right-wing" response to the challenge of Flew and others. Traditional believers will be reassured by the appealing simplicity of Crombie's theory. For example, one can test any statement about God from the religious experiences in the life of a believer which they know to be the attribute of God verified in and by Christ. However, critics have pointed out that the entire theory is based on the willingness of the believer to accept the authority of the Bible as the basis for the ultimate meaningfulness of parabolic affirmation.

Alasdair MacIntyre, the co-editor with Flew of *New Essays* and a "left-wing" philosopher of religion who wants to retain religion and religious language regardless of the nonverifiability or nonfalsifiability of theological utterances, argues in *Metaphys-*

ical Beliefs that the theologian should not attempt to defend religious claims as empirically verifiable or falsifiable. Furthermore, according to MacIntyre, the philosopher of religion should not be concerned with an account of religion that would make it logically reputable. Rather, it is the task of the philosopher to exhibit how, in fact, religious language is used. When analytic philosophers show the illusory character of allegedly metaphysical claims, they provide a valuable service to theology. Such a critique of metaphysics, notes MacIntyre, clears the way for exhibiting the distinctive nature of religious claims.[38]

MacIntyre carefully investigates the nature of religious statements by considering what kind of justification would be appropriate to their logical status as religious beliefs. He shows that religion is hardly a science and therefore cannot be examined by criteria and methods used in that field. For example, religious beliefs are not "explanatory hypotheses." They cannot be justified the way natural science justifies explanatory hypotheses, and to regard them as such is to mistake both the kind of belief they are and the appropriate manner in which they are to be held. Actually, MacIntyre insists that the way religious beliefs are justified is not to ask for or to give reasons. This would be logically inappropriate to the distinctive nature of religious beliefs. Indeed, to ask for such a justification indicates that one has not understood what religious belief is.

For MacIntyre, religion is a special, self-contained area of human concern to be examined and explained within its own criteria—faith and authority—for example, faith in the authority of Jesus Christ. Thus, according to MacIntyre, all religious beliefs are to be justified by referring to authority, and every religion, at least in part, is characteristically defined in terms of what it accepts as an authoritative criterion. Christianity, for example, appeals to Christ as the authority establishing its theological beliefs. Christ's teachings are in turn grounded on the authority of the disciples. Here, notes MacIntyre, the appeal to authority must rest its case or otherwise acknowledge its circularity.[39]

In sum, he says, "We ought not . . . to be surprised that to accept religious belief is a matter not of argument but of conversion."[40] MacIntyre does suggest that talk about God is applying religious myths, using stories about the acts of God in relation to a person's life. He seems to go beyond both Hare and Braithwaite, however, in that for him the believer is committed as much to believing the stories as to acting in accordance with their prescriptions for behavior. Indeed, such stories tell us something about the universe, and MacIntyre therefore concludes that "the religious believer commits himself in his use of myth to the view that these stories are in some way or other stories about a real being, God, acting in the world that we are acquainted with in ordinary experience."[41]

One of MacIntyre's more controversial claims involves the religious believer's refusal to let *anything* count against his beliefs, including the investigation of history. He insists that everything crucial to religious faith cannot be either established or refuted by historical investigation. Whatever historical researchers could turn up about the tomb of Jesus, for example, would not affect a believer's faith in the Resurrection of Jesus Christ. Such a belief is founded on faith and authority, and to such "an act of God historical inquiry is irrelevant."[42] Mitchell later offered a telling criticism of MacIntyre in an article he published entitled "The Justification of Religious Beliefs,"[43] showing that historical inquiry is relevant to belief in historical events. Yet MacIntyre's thesis of a unique logical status for religious language as intelligible only in its own context and with a logic springing from faith and commitment is a popular position. Thus he concludes Part V, "The only apologia for a religion is to describe its content in detail: and then either a man will find himself brought to say 'My Lord and my God' or he will not."[44]

Mitchell has much support for his criticism of MacIntyre

on the subject of MacIntyre's rejection of historical inquiry
as a major criterion of the religious beliefs which arise from
historical events. Indeed, there is something here that reminds
one of Hume's intractability on the subject of any testimony
to support a miraculous event. Further, even those who hold
many of his "left-wing" positions with varying enthusiasm have
called his general theory simplistic and unhelpful to either
extreme.

C. American Naturalist Analyses of Theological Language

Naturalism has long been identified with materialism in both
philosophical and common language use. This confusion is no
longer tenable and several schools of theology have been established which emphasize a theological naturalism. Such a wider
interpretation of naturalism maintains the original method of
inquiry of primitive naturalism, thus religious naturalists accept
data from anything which can be experienced, religion and
God along with history and society, as part of the infinite quantity and quality of nature. It is in this wider view of naturalism
that we now turn to examine the analyses of Henry Nelson
Wieman and John Herman Randali, Jr.

Henry Nelson Wieman of the Divinity School of the University of Chicago is considered by many scholars to be the outstanding contributor to the empirical tradition in theology.[45]
Wieman characterized his own work in an enlightening introductory article which he wrote for a volume in the "Library
of Living Theology," *The Empirical Theology of Henry Nelson
Wieman,* "Intellectual Autobiography."[46] Wieman begins by
noting, "My intellectual life has been focused on a single problem . . . . What operates in human life with such character
and power that it will transform man as he cannot transform
himself . . . ? . . . Transformation can occur only in the form
of events and . . . transformation . . . from them. Therefore
if the religious problem be as stated, theology must be
empirical."[47] Wieman admits to some change in his "focus

of inquiry" from speculation about the universe to "what operates in human life. . . ." He concludes, "Therefore . . . in the actual processes of human existence, must be found the saving and transforming power which religious inquiry seeks and which faith must apprehend."[48] Clearly, since divine revelation is known in the form of events, and events are "distinguished in no other way than by sense experience. Therefore, Christian theology is based on sense experience, otherwise it is unfaithful to original Christianity." Further,

the problem of sense experience for religious inquiry and . . . devotion . . . is to develop it in such a way that it calls forth all the creative powers of human life in profound perceptions. Peter, after *hearing* the words and *seeing* the behavior of Jesus, cries: Thou art the Christ, the Son of the living God. This came out of sense, and without sense experience there is no revelation of God according to the Christian faith.[49]

Numerous critics of Wieman have called attention to his commitment to the metaphysics of naturalism which operates as a set of presuppositions supporting Wieman's empiricism. His naturalism affords a broad concept of nature, however, including processes in man, the universe and God, who Wieman seems to believe functions within nature. Others have claimed that Wieman is also a materialist in that the naturalistic process, while based on a spiritual metaphysics, is nonetheless material. Wieman, replying to such criticism, says, "The religious naturalism I defend is based on the transformation of the mind by interchange with other individuals. This is called naturalism, because it occurs in space and time and is not caused by anything outside of space and time so far as we know."[50] Further, Wieman, in another place, insists that the religious naturalist as described by Wieman identifies the divine presence with the creativity that may occur in the interchange between human beings. The commitment of religious faith, then, sustains and contributes to this creative and distinctively human level of existence in all of its various manifestations.[51] On the subject of materialism, Wieman's writings explain his notion of a reli-

gious "something more." It is in terms of this notion of the
"something more" that Wieman sharply distinguishes the materialism of religious naturalism from everything that was called
materialism in the past. Unlike previous materialisms, Wieman's version does not propose that inanimate matter, as commonly understood, creates all else. Also, religious naturalism
regards quality as objective fact, an ultimate reality. Indeed,
quality as conceived by Wieman is not adjectival to some kind
of underlying featureless and homogenous matter, but the world
is essentially and substantively quality.[52]

Considerable criticism of Wieman, attached to his unsupported naturalistic presuppositions and his latent materialism,
has continued in the face of his enthusiastic apologia. Nevertheless, Wieman remains vulnerable on at least two of his major
positions. First, his use of "nature" is just as ambiguous as
the theist's use of "God," for instance as used in the slogan
"nature is value producing." But what does the word "nature"
mean precisely, and can it be applied to such an endeavor
without the application of faith in a presumed meaning? Second,
Wieman has been criticized for his inadequate characterization
of God, e.g., as "the growth of meaning and value in the world,"
or as "the creative event," or as "creative goodness." The
major criticism here is simply the lack of differentiation between
a God within the system of nature and the Judeo-Christian
God who creates the system of nature and supplies the foundation for value judgment. Yet Wieman must be respected as a
philosophical theologian whose religious statements are consistent with his basic premises and the evidence available to support them.

John Herman Randall, Jr., a former Woodbridge Professor
of Philosophy at Columbia, has made a noteworthy contribution
to the discussions of the Anglo-American empirically oriented
philosophy of religion. His work is of special interest in the
way he builds upon Wieman's naturalism and pragmatism to
expound a noncognitive theory of religious language. Randall
identifies naturalism, in the strictest sense, as a metaphysical

position by which he seeks to exhibit the relation of man and all human experiences to the universe. Human experiences themselves are interpreted as reponses to the powers of the universe or the world in which man is a part. Hence, according to Randall, religious naturalism regards human experience itself as both a revelation of the world in which man discovers himself as well as a revelation of his own powers. By placing human experience squarely within Nature, we more readily exhibit otherwise hidden dimensions of human reality through the exploration of its causes and conditions and its connections to the rest of the world. In addition, the nature of the world itself is further illumined through its relation to human experience. What the world contains is revealed in terms of the many dimensions which are disclosed through human experience. Thus, notes Randall, the world and human experience are all of one piece and mutually illumine each other. This is why, concludes Randall, the fully rounded naturalistic approach will both regard human experience in its natural context as a way to understand religion and equally treat man's actual and concrete religious experience as a way to understand certain aspects of the nature of the universe.[53]

Randall is quick to point out that naturalism (at least his brand), is not opposed to supernaturalism, but rather is concerned to locate within the universe men who do experience its natural place. Randall notes that naturalism has a wider concern than humanism, which supplies mostly a temper or attitude. The naturalist envisions religious experience as an encounter between natural powers and human powers. Religious symbols, then, as understood by the naturalists, function so as to both evoke and organize those nonhuman natural powers which inevitably appear as "superhuman" powers. Religious symbols, since they will not always refer to the powers of man, indeed have to do with what is transcendently experienced from man's point of view as transcendent.[54]

Randall then proceeds to his main thesis that such a "naturalistic" way of understanding religion regards, without exception,

all ideas about God as religious symbols. Furthermore, these
ideas as symbols are only properly grasped in the context of
religious practice. Randall's view of religious symbols, as he
himself acknowledged, has been strongly influenced by the
existential and phenomenologically oriented account of symbols
given by Paul Tillich.[55] Randall begins his own explanation
by drawing a distinction between a symbol and a sign. However,
unlike Tillich, Randall says that only signs are representative,
"a sign of something else." Symbols, on the other hand, are
independent agents which provoke a characteristic response.
Further, while some symbols are cognitive (those in science
and mathematics) many are noncognitive (religious, social and
artistic symbols).

Randall explains the nature of noncognitive symbols in terms
of four often interrelated functions they perform. First, they
address the will rather than the intellect, calling us to commitment and action. Secondly, they may create cooperative activity
or a community of shared concern by eliciting common responses among individuals. Thirdly, it is often the case that
they express and communicate what may be very ambiguous,
or barely conscious, shared experiences. Religious symbols in
this vein are often expressed through art objects. Finally, religious symbols do disclose something about the world out of
which they arise. According to Randall, when religious beliefs
or ideas function as intellectual religious symbols, the issue
of the meaning of religious knowledge is often raised.[56]

Randall insists, however, that such "knowledge" is more
like "insight" or "vision," and concludes that such symbols
do not provide us with verifiable information about any state
of affairs. What they are able to do is to make us "see" some
global or pervasive dimension of the world in which they function. Randall then calls attention to Ernest Cassier's notion
of "symbolic interpretation" in understanding persons, especially as symbolic words and acts convey what are now only
possibilities latent in his nature. Such a symbolic reference

to a person's nature is meaningful since no individual can be reduced solely to what he has already done. Insights into a person's nature, expressed symbolically, then tell us what he can do, and in this sense refer to something more than can be identified with any existing matter of fact or his past behavior.[57] Randall also develops an aesthetic analogy to illustrate how men find the Divine or see visions of God as they find meaning and expression in the arts. Of course, such symbolic language bears no implication that the Divine or God exists. Such a word or concept is only "an intellectual symbol for the religious dimension of the world, for the Divine . . . a quality to be discriminated in human experience of the world [sic.], the splendor of the vision that sees beyond the actual into the perfected and eternal realm of the imagination."[58]

Obviously, Randall is open to some of the general criticisms leveled against religious naturalism, e.g., the foundation of unsupported metaphysical beliefs and the less-than-adequate way naturalists attempt to find a place for God in their theories. Randall works hard to relieve the sting of both criticisms. His naturalism is not quite so impersonal as that of Wieman, since Randall insists that experience of the world and human experience are all of one piece. Further, Randall's theory of religious language as symbolic does help with theological statements that are not cognitively verifiable by showing that they do reveal meaning and express reality. But his use of "noncognitive" to describe symbols is questionable or mistaken. Critics have also voiced concern about Randall's reticence to call religious (and aesthetic) judgments "true," suggesting rather, "reveal," "express," or "teach," since religion is but one art among many. Such critics are not content with the creation of expressive symbols, they insist that religion does provide truth and knowledge. And in the end, it has been suggested that Randall's criticism of Dewey's philosophy of religion, "the husk of religious life without penetrating to the core of Christianity" can be turned back onto himself.[59]

D. American Philosophical Analyses of Theological Language

It was inevitable that the dynamic and influential British movement of analytic philosophy would be exported to the United States and Canada. Further, the growing number of British practitioners of the philosophical analyses of theological language produced such a revolution in the way of doing philosophy of religion and theology that their American counterparts began both to analyze their works and study with them to profit from their endeavors and achievements. In this section we will examine the analyses of Frederick Ferré, Paul van Buren, Donald D. Evans and Dallas M. High, four such American pioneers.

Frederick Ferré, Professor of Philosophy at the University of Georgia, is the first American philosopher to provide a book giving a comprehensive picture of the growth and development of analytic philosophy "as it bears on theological discourse," and "concerning modern methods in philosophy as they relate to the logical nature and validity of theological affirmations." And while Ferré relates the movement of analytic philosophy to British empiricism and logical positivism, he virtually abandons the latter term, quoting Ayer, who wrote that "the Vienna Circle, as a movement, is a thing of the past. So, in a way, is logical positivism. But many of its ideas live on."[60] Ferré also opts for what he calls "functional analysis," or the ordinary language analysis of the later Wittgenstein, Ryle and others; in contrast to what he calls "verificational analysis," or the strict verification principle and the positivist's "veto," described earlier (pp. 59–62). J. A. Martin, Jr., called Ferré's book "one of the wisest and most comprehensive assessments of the significance of analytic philosophy for Christian theology which has yet appeared."[61]

Ferré devotes several chapters to a thorough review of most of the important literature of British philosophical theology discussing the "logic" and "limits" of verificational analysis as well as the "logic" of functional analysis; considering such

terms as analogy, obedience (a term central to neoorthodoxy)
and encounter (a term central to liberalism). He then analyzes
the "improper," the "familiar" and the "unique" functions
of theological discourse and concludes by outlining his own
position under the heading of "The Manifold Logic of Theism."
It is this concluding chapter which will occupy most of our
attention following the statement of Ferré's major thesis—that
religious language may be said to be meaningful. He argues
that theological discourse is regarded as meaningless only if
it is treated like a scientific explanation and then subjected
to the verificational analysis which is tailored to the require-
ments of validity as constituted in the natural sciences. But
once it is recognized that verificational analysis does not define
the only way validity and a rational enterprise may be constituted, then it is not theological language that is found lacking
but verificational analysis.

Ferré is convinced that an analysis of what he calls the
"signification situation" will help to dispel one of the sources
of much confusion in theological discourse. A signification situation occurs when an utterance purports to signify a state of
affairs, a fact of some kind, or something that is the case.
Every signification situation, notes Ferré, contains three factors.
First, there is the factor of the language itself. Secondly, there
must be a language user or interpreter. And of course, the
content signified or that to which the language refers is the
third factor.[62] Each factor, according to Ferré, may provide a
focus for three different theoretical approaches—each perhaps
with its own criterion of validity—to the signification-situation.
Thus there are: syntactics (the study of language in terms of
the more formal relationships and properties of verbal signs);
"interpretics" (Ferré's word for the relationship between language and the user-interpreter); and semantics (the study of
language in terms of the relationship between language and
its referent). From this consideration of the three factors and
elements (or dimensions) of language, Ferré concludes: "One
of the major sources of confusion concerning the analysis of

theological discourse is a failure to distinguish the three dimensions of the signification-situation as they arise in the full, concrete functioning of theological language."[63]

Ferré now turns to the question of assessing the three dimensions of theological language. The "syntactical" analysis is accomplished by references to the "internal language norms" of religious statements according to what Ferré calls "equivalences" (of terms) and "entailment" of the "informal" logic of theology. The analysis of "interpretics" emphasizes the effect of religious language on the user-interpreter as well as the "active" way in which the user-interpreters use religious language for a purpose. This analysis is so important that Ferré declares that, without a comprehension of the interpretive function of its language, no understanding of theism is possible. However, it is the "semantical" analysis which Ferré chooses as the most complete and responsible assessment of religious language, the investigation of the ontological status of the referent of theological statements. He says that they are completely misunderstood unless they are regarded as referring to the nature of reality, which is to say, some state of affairs or facts of some kind. Indeed, according to Ferré, theologians in the final analysis must acknowledge that the semantic reference of discourse about God is to some kind of metaphysical fact.

Ferré, unlike the logical positivists, regards the notion of a metaphysical fact as meaningful. Indeed, he expounds the significance of metaphysical facts in terms of a comparison with scientific facts. Both scientific and metaphysical facts are products of experience as well as the conceptual activity of the mind. In the case of scientific facts, however, their significance is overwhelmingly established by conceptually organized experience and their key position within the often intricate theoretical structures of the sciences. How these facts are defined depends both on the way they mesh with other facts and on the precision of theoretical constructions. Should there be persistent shortcomings on either side, this would eventually call forth a reconsideration of whatever counts for the "facts."

Such reconsiderations are a major undertaking and signal the kind of revolutions in science that are relatively infrequent. Metaphysical "facts" are a kind of second-order scientific fact, according to Ferré. Thus, metaphysical facts are components of a conceptual synthesis which attempts to create a superordinate matrix in terms of which all the facts are granted a coherence. The theoretical model as metaphysical construct, however, is drawn from among the "facts" disclosed by science. A strictly defined metaphysical fact, then, is a concept which plays a crucial role within the system, a concept without which the system would collapse.[64] Further, Ferré claims that he has come around to the opinion that criteria can be found for rationally assessing metaphysical systems: internally by consistency and coherences; and externally by applicability to experience and adequacy to *all* possible experience.

Ferré concludes that "roughly speaking . . . to say that theological discourse refers to 'metaphysical fact' is equivalent to asserting that theological language *on its semantic dimension* functions as metaphysical language." He then sketches the function of theistic models as a species of metaphysical language. Theology conveys a model of immense responsive significance. Its crucial components are drawn from the facts of human personality which have to do with will, purpose, wisdom, love and the like. In Christianity, the conceptual synthesis of these aspects of human life is achieved in the model of Christ's life as one of creative, self-giving, personal love. For Christians, the model of Christ's life contains the only literal meaning which terms like "personal," "creative" and "love" can have in the Christian vocabulary. The model of Christ serves as the center around which all the concepts of Christian life are arrayed. The task of systematic theology, notes Ferré, is to exhibit and explain the coherence and consistency of the synthesis built on this model of "God" as the crucial concept. Christian preaching is concerned with helping the believer to apply this conceptual synthesis to his own life. And Christian apologetics, according to Ferré, strives to show that the interpretation of

life's meaning organized around this model is adequate to capture in an unforced way all the drama of interpersonal life,
including suffering and evil.[65]

Ferré's identification of theological discourse with a legitimate kind of metaphysical language embodies an attempt on
his part to take seriously the ontological status of what tradition-
ally has been regarded as God's transcendence. In this regard,
Ferré cites with approval Dorothy Emmet's remark on the ontological significance of the theologian as metaphysician.

> Religious thinking may well have other concerns besides the epistemolog-
> ical question of the relation of our ideas to reality beyond ourselves.
> But here, if anywhere, this question cannot be avoided, since religion
> loses its nerve when it ceases to believe that it expresses in some way
> truth about our relation to a reality beyond ourselves which ultimately
> concerns us.[66]

Ferré's account of religious discourse, then, remains true to
the resolution of faith not to "lose its nerve" in the face of
twentieth-century secularism's tendency to deny the reality of
a transcendent God. By insisting that his identification of God
with a metaphysical model of personal activity will best survive
any tests which may be demanded, Ferré preserves theism's
traditional belief in the independent being of God.[67] And for
this Ferré has earned the appreciation of many theologians
and laymen.

Ferré also has won the plaudits of philosophical theologians
not only as the first American to enter into dialogue with the
philosophical analysts, but also because he demonstrated the
relevance of their tools and techniques for theological explanation. Further, he is to be congratulated on moving beyond
both the syntactic and interpretive analyses of theological language to consider the "internal logic" of the actual language
used in an actual religious community. However, Ferré's theory
of a "conceptual synthesis" as the grounds to support a theological model similar to a scientific model drawn from the facts,
both empirical and metaphysical, fails to explain any more

than we already know—that theology is similar to metaphysics.

Paul M. van Buren, Professor in the Department of Religion at Temple University, is without doubt the most widely read empiricist-analytic practitioner of philosophical theology in the United States. Much of this notoriety was caused by his being linked with the architects of the "God is dead" movement in the United States by *Time* magazine in a cover story in the 1960s. However, his book, *The Secular Meaning of the Gospel*, is much more important than the popularization of its "secular" implications. Actually "secular" means "empirical" and indicates van Buren's conversion and commitment to the empiricism represented by Ayer and Flew to whom *empirical* meant verifiable or falsifiable. Van Buren's characteristically analytic standpoint, a stance which separates him from the radical theologians is indicated in his declaration: "Today we cannot even understand the Nietzschian cry that 'God is dead!' for if it were so, how could we know? No, the problem now is that the *word* 'God' is dead."[68]

Van Buren undertakes an important study of the various expressions of "the concern for Christology," from Chalcedon to "secular Christianity," one segment of which is a helpful discussion of the contributions of other analysts of religious language. He concludes that the term "God" is literally meaningless in our secular-empirical mood and thus takes his stand with Flew. It is not that the empiricist, notes van Buren, has difficulty in making sense out of what is said about God, but rather the consistent empiricist finds the entire enterprise of talking about God as problematic. This is so since the empiricist does not know what God is and consequently has no way of understanding how the term "God" is employed. Apparently, points out van Buren, it functions as a name and yet theologians constantly remind us that we cannot use it as we customarily employ names in order to refer to something specific. Should the term "God" be intended to refer to an "existential attitude," the attitude of the speaker, or his self-understanding, then surely, complains van Buren, a clearer and more appropriate

expression could be found. However, van Buren warns us that
the problem will not be solved by merely substituting some
other word for the term "God." The difficulty lies as much
in how the term is used, whether it be "God" or "X," as it
does with any attempted explicit definition of the term. The
task of linguistic analysis then, in a secular age, is to confront
squarely this problem of the logic of the apparently meaningless
theistic language contained in the gospel.[69] Van Buren also
takes his stand with Hare and Braithwaite by choosing "a
non-cognitive, 'blik' conception of faith, rather than of a cognitive conception . . . [as] fundamental to our study." He explains
that the cognitive approach to religious language would contradict the honestly secular starting point of contemporary empiricism. The cognitive approach must be resisted because it tends
to divide experience into the secular and the sacred, and then
suggest that there is a special way of knowing the sacred or
religious as opposed to other or secular ways of knowing. In
this way the cognitive approach is ill-suited to the ultimate
presuppositions of secular thought and to the heart of the gospel
as well. As far as van Buren is concerned, thoroughly secular
interpreters of the gospel must all agree that "simple literal
theism" is wrong and that "qualified literal theism" is meaningless.[70]

Still, van Buren maintains that linguistic analysis can clarify
the noncognitive function of religious language. By first criticizing those explanations of religious discourse which allege to
identify this language with cosmological assertions, analysis
then clears the way for exhibiting the prescriptive function
of religious discourse in relation to the practices of Christian
life. He concludes by acknowledging that the force of the problems generated by contemporary philosophical reflection on
the language of faith is felt so strongly just because many
have adopted a frankly empirical method which reflects the
thinking of an industrialized, scientific age. By remaining un-
qualifiably consistent with the empirical approach, analysts have
discovered that the oblique theologies of modern theism are

no better off, and sometimes worse, than the simple literal theism of bygone days. There is no way of avoiding, notes van Buren, the moral exasperation of Flew's skeptical explorer if we are to attempt to understand the gospel today.[71]

Van Buren offers a substitute for the elimination of words about God in theology, a dynamic Christology based on a Jesus who represents a man unique in his faith, freedom and love. Van Buren's account of the Easter Gospel illustrates his equation of faith and freedom. The disciples, suggests van Buren, discerned in Jesus a new way of relating to one another and indeed to the whole world. From the moment they experienced this way of seeing Jesus, they began to possess the same freedom Jesus exhibited. The freedom of Jesus became contagious and because the disciples experienced this freedom as a new life, their story of Jesus had to include the event of Easter. Thus, according to van Buren, the Easter story, once we get over treating it as a report of a natural or supernatural resuscitation of Jesus' corpse, is really the climax of the story of how the free man Jesus sets other men free.[72]

Van Buren suggested two principles for the proclamation of the gospel message in secular times:

(1) *Statements of faith are to be interpreted, by means of the modified verification principle, as statements which express, describe, or commend a particular way of seeing the world, other men, and oneself, and the way of life appropriate to such a perspective.*

(2) *The norm of the Christian perspective is the series of events to which the New Testament documents testify, centering in the life, death, and resurrection of Jesus of Nazareth.*[73]

Van Buren later admitted to some significant changes in his earlier position in *Theological Explorations* (1968) mainly in a modification of his rigid use of the verification principle, allowing that meaningful language is defined by usage and that metaphysical statements functioned as proposals suggesting "how things are." However, in 1972 van Buren published *The Edges of Language*, which helped to dethrone verificational analysis and the positivist's veto, and established new models for understanding theological language. One model is a flat earth with theological statements at the edges of language, along with humor, metaphysics and paradox, where all are in danger of falling off (into nonsense). After a re-examination of the several theories and interpretations of religious language, van Buren accepts Ferré's notion of "functional analysis" and notes that such analysis shows that our religious statements express the way we live. He argues that "decisions about language are decisions about life and changing our ways of speaking changes our way of life."[74]

Van Buren finally examines the development of "words about God" and now admits that he was mistaken in *Secular Meaning* to argue that the word "God" was dead. Instead he now wishes to affirm that: "A desire, a longing to push out the limits of some particular area of our language, implies that there is a realm of discourse and life in which our ordinary, or rule-governed, behavior does not seem to be adequate."[75] Van Buren seems now to hold that the word "God" can yet indicate today what it did in the past if we understand that the term refers to that which lies on the very boundary of language. Talk of "God" is the religious way of indicating that one aspires to say all that could possibly be said on some matter of great concern. Such an enterprise, notes van Buren, lies just barely but legitimately within our language.[76]

Van Buren is the American counterpart of the British left-wing philosophical theologians and his *Secular Meaning* reveals his very strict interpretation of the logical positivists' verification principle even in the face of some damaging criticisms which had been presented on both sides of the Atlantic. Based on stringent verificational analysis, van Buren rejects all forms of God-talk and proposes a special Christologically centered form of religious language with an accompanying humanist-naturalist theology. Thus critics have asked, How is Jesus-talk possible without God-talk? Other critics have blamed van Buren's revolutionary theory of religious language on his inadequate theory of language in general. And some have pointed out that van Buren's supporting arguments are often vague and inconclusive.

Donald D. Evans is an Oxford-trained Professor of Philosophy at Toronto University who acknowledges the influence of Ian T. Ramsey in his book, *The Logic of Self-Involvement.* [77] Evans sees his own work as a further development and application of certain themes suggested by J. L. Austin's discussion of "performative language." Specifically, Evans employs Austin's notion of the performative function of a linguistic event in order to clarify the phenomena of self-involving language. He also goes on to show that this performative function often plays a crucial role in religious language.

Austin had made a considerable contribution to analytic philosophy by his analysis of speech acts, of the meaningful things we do when we speak—e.g., stating, ordering, promising, and so on. Austin's *How to Do Things with Words*, published posthumously, called attention to three levels of speech acts: locutions, or the act *of* stating meaningful sentences; illocutions, or what we are doing *in* speaking, stating, ordering, promising; and perlocutions, or what we are doing *by* speaking, informing, urging, warning. From these distinctions, which established the importance of performative language as illocutions, Austin classified five illocutionary speech acts. Evans lists these as: constantives or expositives (utterances which state something and as Evans adds can be true or false and give meaning), commissives (promising or acts of commitment), exercitives (exercising a power, e.g., enacting, commissioning, and so on), behabitives (involving attitudes or social behavior), and verdictives (giving of verdicts or other judgments).

Evans did in fact modify Austin's methodology and categories. For example, he points out in a footnote that his use of "constantive" in place of Austin's "expositive" is a major revision, since Evans now insists that constantives are "true-or-false (or accurate or inaccurate, or correct-or-incorrect, and so on). In contrast with this, Austin criticizes the use of any such criterion for classifying utterances; and he does not use any such criterion when he distinguishes his class of Expositives."[78] Evans then develops his theory of "self-involving" language. His summary of the theory in "Differences Between Scientific and Religious Assertions" is clear and persuasive. Basically, Evans suggests that religious assertions are always a species of self-involving assertions, while scientific assertions are not. He defines a self-involving assertion as one which commits the person who states it or believes it to further action, or at least implies that he has a definite attitude for or against the asserted claim. Evans offers as examples of self-involving asser- tions the following: "I promise to return this book tomorrow," "I commend Jones for his restraint," and "I look on you as a father." In each of these cases, Evans points out, "I" *cannot* deny the self-involvement. Here the force of the "cannot" is logical in character. The logical status of the self-involvement is what Austin had intended when he designated this kind of linguistic utterance as performative. The performative meaning depends usually on public linguistic and institutional conven- tions. Sometimes, notes Evans, it also depends on special con- texts of meaning or on the eccentric or special intentions of the speaker.[79]

But for Evans, language is also performative in other ways. For example, it is expressive of feelings and of attitudes. And Evans performs a thorough analysis of the language, expressing both feelings and attitudes to provide an adequate and accurate map of these complex concepts. Evans noted that "most lan- guage is to some extent expressive" (poetry is primarily expres- sive) even though on the other extreme, scientific statements are highly impersonal.[80] He differentiates between feelings and attitudes showing that attitudes contain much more than one's feelings, e.g., opinions, intentions and behavior. Evans points out that while feelings are for the most part immediate and relatively transitory, attitudes on the other hand embody more stable dispositions and express conscious relations to other per- sons or things. Thus, more specifically, attitudes involve being for or against something or someone. They convey a regard for someone or something as important or unimportant.

Evans's important contribution to the field of religious language is his notion of "onlook," or the expression by an individual or group of the total self-involving performative use of language. He says, "I have coined the word 'onlook' as a substantive for what it is to 'look on x as y,' "[81] and he adds that "onlooks" do possess some common features: commissive, autobiographical, expressive, behavitive-postural, and verdictive. Some onlooks are literal, some nonliteral (parabolical, analogical or metaphysical), yet they are an important part of our everyday language, e.g., "I look on every human being as a person."[82]

Evans concludes that "religious belief is the conviction (or hope) that one's onlook conforms to an authoritative onlook, a divine onlook. We shall see that biblical belief in world-Creation includes the belief that God has *prescribed* a role and status for men and has *appraised* human existence positively."[83] The remainder of Evans's book is an illustration of the application of performative language, his theory of self-involvement, and his concept of "onlook" to the biblical doctrine of Creation. He concludes that only the complex pattern of biblical or quasi-biblical onlooks can provide an adequate interpretive context for the self-involving confession of faith in God the Creator.

Evans has made a considerable contribution to the field of philosophical theology by his use of the helpful language category suggested by Austin of performatives (or performative utterance). Further, he combined the influence of Austin with that of Ramsey to show that religious language is intimately related to attitudes and self-involvement and seeks to evoke personal commitment. Also, with Ramsey, Evans holds to a differentiating quality which defines a peculiar dimension in our experience and thus to the language describing this experience appropriate to that special dimension. Evans's weaknesses are a latent vagueness and imprecision in explaining many of his key terms and an overall prescriptive stance in applying Austin's performative language category to biblical theology.

Dallas M. High is an American philosopher of religion trained at Duke University. He is relevant to this study because of his agreement with, and use of, Evans's concept of self-involvement. Further, he agrees with and uses Ramsey's emphasis on personalism and the importance to religious language of the individual, the person, the "I" who speaks God-talk. Moreover, High, like Ramsey, has been influenced strongly by the recent work in philosophy of Wittgenstein and his followers. Both, following Wittgenstein's lead, construe empiricism in a much broader fashion than the logical positivists or those like Ayer who championed verificational analysis. As for High himself, he explains the major thesis of his book, *Language, Persons and Belief,* in his preface as "an attempt to explore some aspects of Wittgenstein's later work and to ascertain its bearing on . . . the area of religious thought and discourse."[84] There is little doubt of High's debt to Wittgenstein, yet Wittgenstein's influence on High's work is not in the same vein that Wittgenstein has influenced other philosophers of religion who have been justly called Wittgenstein "fideists" by some critics. The title "fideist" is taken from the acceptance (incorrectly) that Wittgenstein separated off several "languages" and noted discrete "language-games" for each, namely ethics, religion, aesthetics, and so on; and thus religious language demands a specific presupposition—faith.

High is not a fideist, but a personalist who insists on the unique importance of the person, the "I" who speaks and uses language following the rules of many language-games. Language, as the medium in which human life expresses itself, becomes nothing but dead marks and scratches on inert matter if it is severed from its personal source. Like Wittgenstein, High insists that words and sentences treated apart from their use are neither meaningful nor meaningless. They only attain these characteristics in the context of their use. It is this approach, seeing that the meaning of ordinary discourse is conferred by use, which when brought to the domain of religious discourse is fruitful for exhibiting how indeed the meaning of religious discourse may be illumined by paying attention to the context in which it is employed.[85]

High adopts another notion put forward by Wittgenstein, that of the concept "form of life." Wittgenstein had written ". . . to imagine a language means to imagine a form of life,"[86] and in another place he insisted that "what has to be accepted, the given, is—so one could say—*forms of life*,"[87] which High suggests "provides the sense and sensibility of our speech . . . [and] likewise, what we understand and count as reality (or the world) is closely connected with the language and human life, particularly our conceptual forms."[88] Unfortunately, neither Wittgenstein nor High makes clear what a form of life is, although High seems to favor "Western culture," to set the norms for the use of language, including the religious use of language. Thus the sense and sensibility of religious language, like that of more ordinary language, can only be understood by looking at its use. However, it is often difficult, as Wittgenstein himself had pointed out, to avoid the prejudices that stand in the way of doing this.

High then analyzes "belief utterances" and more specifically introduces the importance of the first person, personal pronoun use as he writes, "Believing is something *performed, owned,* and *claimed by,* for someone, *about* and *in* someone or something."[89] This expresses for High the primacy of believing over beliefs, and the person who believes over what is believed. Such an emphasis on first-person belief utterances would cure the intellectual malaise caused by the third-person type in which the meaning of beliefs have been mistakenly identified by some as that which can be treated in terms of the test procedures of third-person, factual-truth conditions. Those who demand that beliefs are to be justified in terms of their connection to factual or descriptive truth conditions are misguided. This, High reminds us, does not mean that belief utterances then have no rationale or that they are immune from every kind of criticism. Theologians who retreat into paradox, irrationality and otherwise oblique accounts of religion out of response to the demands of the third-person model of the conditions of meaningful belief-utterances are equally wrongheaded, according to High. They inflict religious faith with an aura of necessary dogmatism.

Finally, in the mode of Evans's "self-involvement" and Ramsey's personalism,[90] High develops his argument for God-talk. He notes that as we do not exhaust the concept of self ("I") in considering simply the observable acts or behavior, so we do not exhaust talk of God by reference to events in the world. Further, High shows how the performance of personal belief as self-involvement—e.g., " 'I' believe in 'you' "—functions as a conceptual model of creedal-doctrinal utterances—e.g., "I believe in God. . . ."[91]

High concludes by noting that he has given reasons for or anchored certain belief-utterances, yet he insists that given the human manner of speaking and reasoning, *neither* evidence for (verification) *nor* evidence against (falsification) is a conclusive guarantee of certitude. He says that the inquiry has been open-ended mainly because it is an inquiry into our own involvement in life and culture. When a philosophical reflection makes us aware of belief utterances in this way it heightens, rather than slackens, our personal claims and allegiances. Such a reflection, furthermore, cannot relieve us of all doubt, suspicion and risk. Indeed, High proposes that such an engagement in life is precisely the character of genuine "believing," "thinking," "reasoning" and "speaking" if it is concerned with anything intelligible at all. And it is High's view that religious belief especially manifests this "engagement" in the human venture.

High may be commended as helpful because of his explanation of Wittgenstein's language game as simply a different usage of ordinary words, not a different set of words, and for his demonstration of the basic relation between usage and meaning within the context of the life situation where meanings are communicated. Further, High is to be lauded for his personal-

ism and his observation of the many senses for God-talk as
well as the many ways of justifying such language. However,
High is guilty of vagueness on some of his important concepts,
e.g., Wittgenstein's "form of life" and his own definition of
person.

E. A Summary and a Look Ahead

A chapter on "Empirical Theology" is important to the thesis
of this book on the Christian empiricism of Ian Ramsey because
it links him without challenge not only to classical and contemporary empiricism, but also with the several movements which
are the result of attempts to apply the tenets of empiricism
to the discipline of theology. We have briefly examined the
contributions of seven British analytic philosophers to the early
dialogue between philosophers and theologians centered mostly
in the universities. Next we considered the analyses of two
American naturalists and reviewed their special claims and
explications. Finally we studied the work of four American
analytic philosophers who also at various times participated
in the dialogue which made empirical theology an accepted
field of theological analysis and explanation. In sum, we have
been confronted with many theories of religious language and
knowledge from "left-wing" noncognitive or humanist-naturalist reductions to "right-wing" objectivist-theist emphases which
would preserve the meaning as well as the personal reference
of God-talk. With this foundation, we now are better prepared
to consider the special conciliatory work of Ramsey since he
is a good example of some elements of empiricism and some
elements of empirical theology. Indeed, there are some who
think Ramsey has made the most significant contribution to
the merger and meaning of this special field, empirical theology.
The next chapter will explore Ramsey's thought and contributions: his concept of the "more," his analysis of "I," his disclosure theory, his theory of qualified models, his case for the
metaphysical, and his concept of "logical fit," in order to understand the claim of Christian empiricism.

IV. A Christian Empiricist:
Empiricism and "More"

A. Introduction

In order to decide whether Ian Ramsey may be called a Christian empiricist, we shall of necessity have to review the similarities of his works and teachings with those of both classical and contemporary philosophical empiricism and with empirical theology as well. In the face of Ramsey's claim for a direct inheritance from philosophical empiricism, we will be able to support only a qualified legacy or what we shall call "situational" empiricism. In the examination of Ramsey's empiricism some of his concepts which he calls empirically grounded, such as the "more" and his analysis of "I," will be scrutinized as possible supports for his notion of a "wider" empiricism. Ramsey's relationship with empirical theology and with the philosophical theologians practicing conceptual analysis is too obvious to question. Therefore we will state and evaluate his unique contributions to the analysis and elucidation of religious language such as the disclosure theory, with its attendant concepts of discernment and commitment, and the theory of qualified models as a helpful explicator of theological statements. Finally we will consider Ramsey's claims and procedures to confirm and justify both the claim of religious knowledge stemming from his "wider" empiricism and the claim of clarity and understanding of the words about God coming from his theories of religious language.

B. A Qualified Inheritance: Ian T. Ramsey's "Situational" Empiricism

1. Ramsey's concept of the "more" and a "wider" or "broader" empiricism

The importance of Ramsey as a philosophical theologian derives from his contribution of a third alternative to the call of logical empiricism to surrender to its "veto" or to the call of neoscholasticism or neoorthodoxy to escape into an empirically free fideism. Unfortunately, his work is hardly a unified whole. It consists of many sketches of his theses in numerous books and articles which are notable not only for an occasional insight into the "Empirical Placing of Theological Phrases" (the subtitle of his main book, *Religious Language*), but also for the many gaps in their reasoning, with only hints at the explanation of his main concern to maintain the empirical cognitivity of religious language.

It is fortunate, however, that there is a growing corpus of literature about Ramsey and his special contributions which does attempt to give a more comprehensive overview. We can be grateful to the many commentators and critics, whose outlines, summaries, integrations, criticisms, commentaries and interpretations make possible an adequate development of the work of a thinker whose untimely death made impossible his own more comprehensive explanations and justifications.[1]

One thing which can be said about Ramsey without fear of dissent is that all of his works and theories show his primary respect for and appreciation of empiricism. Further, as a committed churchman and theologian, Ramsey also wished to develop an account of religious discourse which, while maintaining its mystical components and depth, would nonetheless be anchored in actual human experience. Edwards tells of Ramsey's remark to Hugh Joseph, a friend, indicating his ambition to "build a bridge between theology and philosophy."[2]

Of course, Ramsey's efforts at bridge-building did not prevent his critical analyses of both theology and philosophy. He warned theologians that:

> We must make plain the empirical anchorage of theological assertions. . . . At the same time, theological assertions must have a logical context which extends to, and is continuous with, those assertions of ordinary language for which sense experience is directly relevant. From such straightforward assertions, theological assertions must not be logically segregated: for that would mean that they were pointless and, in contrast to the only language which has an agreed meaning, meaningless.[3]

At the same time Ramsey rejected the positivist's "veto" of religious language and theology and insisted on a "wider" or "broader" empiricism which would allow philosophic consideration of religious experience and discourse.

According to C. H. Dodd, Ramsey's reason for going to Oxford from Cambridge was to meet the challenge of those who claimed that religious propositions were nonsense. Ramsey's aim, while at Oxford, was to master the new analytic philosophy so that he might employ its very methods to demonstrate the arbitrariness and limits of its presuppositions. In this way, he hoped to construct an apologetic that would meet head on the criticisms analytic philosophy directed against Christianity. Ramsey's studies at Oxford, notes Dodd, provide a notable example of a man setting himself to prepare the role he was to fulfill.

As it happened Ramsey did make some essential modifications of the popular logical empiricist concept of "empirical" which he noted in the teaching of John Locke. In his Introduction to *The Reasonableness of Christianity* (when he edited the book in 1958), Ramsey, referring to the diminishing prestige of metaphysics in providing theological explanations, asks:

> Can we find in Locke, as the founder of eighteenth-century empiricism, some hints as to where the narrower empiricism of some of his successors is inadequate, and where also a broader empiricism might do more justice to the reasonableness and distinctiveness of the Christian faith than was ever possible when metaphysics of the old brand held sway? Here is the timeliness of Locke for our own day.[4]

It was empiricism in the broad sense—advocated by Locke—that Ramsey adopted. As did Locke, so Ramsey seems to allow an "inner sense" to add data to the other senses in the determination of meaning and verification.

Thus developed the influential notion in Ramsey's theories of the "more." It is obviously not Ramsey's invention, for H. N. Wieman, following William James, insisted on a "more" in experience not reducible to human behavior, yet not a *sui generis* supernatural concept. Both noted a "more" in every event or experience which might become discernible from a "gestalt" of occurrences and experiences. Ramsey calls on the "more" to answer the logical empiricists' contempt for religious language and their dictum that all meaningful language is either empirical (in the narrow sense of Hume, Ayer and Flew) or tautological (an analytical truth: a brother is a male sibling).

Early in *Religious Language*, Ramsey announced his thesis that religion is ultimately based on experiences wherein one discerns in a unique way that there is a "more" or a depth implicit to a visible and spatio-temporal situation which, though unseen, is experienced as essential.[5] Later in *Christian Discourse* he noted two oft-heard complaints. "The one . . . is that contemporary philosophy is a soul-destroying verbalism. The other . . . made by the same people—is that theology is vacuous chatter, a hollow sham, a bogus pretence, a jungle through which no logical paths may be mapped." In the Riddell Memorial Lectures of 1933, Ramsey allied himself with the approach of analytic philosophy and argued that both of the above complaints could be dismissed once analysis was employed as an apologetic instrument for religious discourse. Analysis, Ramsey proposed, would help to clarify the intricacies of theological arguments and thus dissolve the logical tangles which often frustrate religious understanding.[6]

Further, Edwards quotes from a sermon to the British Association at Durham Cathedral delivered in 1970 in which Ramsey points to the need for an empirical anchor for theology.

> The main mistake [is] to suppose that theology is prescriptive, dictating the answers to which scientific inquiry must come. But the distinctive function of theology is . . . to witness to "depth," . . . to take seriously the moral dimension. . . . Theology needs to do a task which it avoided doing for some three hundred years; and deliberately refused to do a hundred years ago. But the road to such an integration, the road to a contemporary mapping or projection of theology, is the same as the road to a scientific culture—through the crucible of contemporary social and moral problems shared by all disciplines.[7]

Ramsey was aware of the criticisms of his fellow philosophers and theologians that his notion of "the more" was either nonsense or occult and issued a demurrer to two popular misconceptions: "that those with an intense affection for ordinary language must necessarily deny metaphysics, or those who defend metaphysics must necessarily trade in occult and shadowy worlds. Which means that the book has been fighting on two battle fronts at once; and, it is a sobering reflection that not many wars have been won under such a necessity."[8] Regardless, Ramsey accepted the challenge and plunged into the warfare on the side of those using empiricist methodologies to reveal the inadequacies of logical empiricism and to show that metaphysics and theology were more than nonsense. He did, however, agree with some of the empiricists' criticisms of metaphysics and theology. For instance, in *Freedom and Immortality* he quotes the libertarians who say that "our timeless self opts for that alternative [freedom]," or that "we are determined by the Moral Law to select that alternative." With C. D. Broad he questions both the intelligibility as well as the truth or falsity of the first observation. Ramsey then questions what the libertarians could possibly mean when they speak of the Moral Law determining anything? Also in *Words About God* he reveals his radical analysis of the more traditional metaphysical-theology by insisting that

> . . . a good deal of the doctrinal controversy of the early church might have been avoided had the Christological problem, for example, been seen to be one of how to use language reliably about Jesus Christ, rather than supposed to be a problem of anthropology or psychology or ontology which asked how two "natures" could be combined into something which, while being completely both, yet was a single homogeneous unity. To phrase the problem in this way is virtually to preclude any intelligible solution.[9]

Thus, for Ramsey, his "wider empiricism" and his concept of the "more" make possible an analysis and a reconstruction of a rational and meaningful use of religious language. In the tradition of the later Wittgenstein and other more flexible analytic philosophers, e.g., J. L. Austin, Max Black and P. F. Strawson, Ramsey applied the logical empiricist's concern for meaning and verification to religious discourse, and hoped to "revitalize our faith and our doctrine and make what seem so often to be the dry bones of theological discourse live."[10]

Here we meet what seems to be a basic paradox in Ramsey's thought: in some ways he continues the radical/left-wing analysis of Braithwaite, Hare, Flew, et. al.; yet he insists, along with the liberal/right-wing views of Mitchell, Ferré, et. al., on the meaningfulness of theological discourse. Ramsey noted his indebtedness to the more flexible analytic philosophers a number of times. Thus, in his book, *Models and Mystery*, Ramsey acknowledged the influence of Black in his own work. In two symposia he acknowledged his interest in Austin's "performative" category of language which revealed a new interest in the personal as being something "more" than descriptive. He also acknowledged that Strawson's book, *Individuals*, had enlightened his own view of personality.

Ramsey's concept of the "more" rectifies the narrow form

of logical empiricism by taking into account dimensions of experience, and this "more" he describes as common to ordinary language as well as to theoretical science and theology. Indeed, he argues that to limit reality to the publicly observable and knowledge to sense experience and logic would not only hamper religious language but also cause difficulties in other language use, notably scientific theory. Ramsey points out interesting relationships between science, religion and the language of theory and explanation in each field. He notes the similarities and differences carefully. The similarities include the basic observability of both as they confront, or are confronted with, empirical facts, the discernment from the observables of a pattern which prompts a hypothesis/generalization and the similar use of ordinary language process. The differences include the extent of the observables, the greater concreteness of scientific language, the focus in science on physical rather than personal phenomena, and the process and success of verification. Ramsey also insists that logical empiricism, modified by his "scientific *and more*" criterion, adds values to religious knowledge and discourse which not only begins in human experience, but also must be constantly analyzed and evaluated to preserve its meaning and sense—a process that could produce revision and change. It is this which causes Ramsey to call religion and science "complementary." And he adds, "Religion can give to science that affirmation of the universe which it needs. . . . [And] science can satisfy religion in its venture after fuller and fuller relevance, after more and more adequate discursive expression. . . . I have suggested that the scientist can only secure his wildest dreams when he becomes religious. At the same time the theologian can only secure his . . . when he becomes scientific."[11]

Having proposed his "broader" concept of empiricism as reality and knowledge grounded in experience, but not limited to public observables and the specific experience itself, Ramsey gives many examples of situations where the "more" may be discerned. Evans has offered a classification which sorts out the somewhat bewildering array of Ramsey's examples of the discernment of "more." Evans's classification includes:

(1) *Awareness of I:*
   (a) *I*, as a conscious subject using language, am more than my describable, observable behaviour. For the subject-object distinction presupposes that there is at least one subject, and all language presupposes a subject using language.
   (b) *I*, as conscious agent, acting in a free or personal or authentic way, in contrast with an involuntary (or conditioned reflex) way, an impersonal (or official) way, or an unauthentic way, am more than my describable, observable behaviour.
(2) *Personal encounter:* The *I* of another human being whom we discern in personal encounter is more than his describable, observable behaviour.
(3) *Moral claim:* A moral claim to which one responds in a situation is more than the situation as described in terms of observables.
(4) *Aesthetic wonder:* An impressive work of art such as a picture, poem or symphony, which evokes wonder, is more than the describable features of the work of art.
(5) *Whole:* A whole is more than the sum of its parts. For example, a gestalt pattern is more than the sum of its parts.
(6) *Scientific models:* What a scientific model is about is more than the observables to which it is applied. For example, electricity as a current is more than what's observed; light as waves or particles is more than what's seen; the opposition of an induced current to a magnet is more than what's observed.
(7) *Infinite mathematical series:* A circle is more than any polygon in an infinite series where each polygon has one more side than the previous polygon. The number 2 is more than any sum in an infinite series "1 plus ½ plus ¼ plus ⅛ plus ¹⁄₁₆ . . . ."
(8) *Concrete particular:* A particular thing in its concrete particularity is more than any list of features on the basis of which we recognize it or identify it.[12]

Evans names (1) (b) as the "central case of the 'more',"
and adds, "the awareness of *I* is the key to all the other
discernments of 'more'. . . ." Evans notes that Ramsey's "I"
is both experienceable and *discernible*, something that is experienced yet something which transcends all descriptions of experi-

ence and behavior. And Evans insists that Ramsey's " 'more' is a form of *activity* rather than a mere happening or movement."[13] Evans then goes on to show that there is a significant overlapping of these classifications and concludes that "paradigm discernments of *I* are correlated with discernments of something *other* than *I* . . . something 'more' than observables . . . self-awareness is correlated with awareness of an external other which, like the self, transcends observables. . . ."[14]

2. *Ramsey's Analysis of "I" or Self-Awareness*

Terrence W. Tilley calls Ramsey a personalist empiricist because of the important role the concept of self plays in Ramsey's thought. Indeed, it is perhaps Ramsey's major thesis that " 'I' will never cease to be a useful guide when we are confronted with puzzles about 'God.' "[15]

Ramsey responded to both David Hume and Gilbert Ryle in the process of establishing his important concept of the "I." As a citadel of the "more" of self-awareness, the "I" is transcendent in the sense that it cannot be contained in scientific discourse, nor reduced to terms of observable behavior. Ramsey criticized Hume's "bundle-theory" of the self which ultimately denied that the self was anything more than a bundle of discrete impressions which happen to be bound together by sequence or contiguity in the mind. Hume denied that there was any discrete impression of self, therefore self is an illusion.

Ramsey quotes Hume's classic account in *A Treatise of Human Nature*, "For my part, when I enter most intimately into what I call *myself*, I always stumble on some particular perception or other, of heat or cold, light or shade, love or hatred, pain or pleasure. I never can catch *myself* at any time without a perception. . . ." From this observation, Hume concludes that he

. . . never can observe anything but the perception. If any one upon serious and unprejudic'd reflexion, thinks he has a different notion of

> *himself*, I must confess I can reason no longer with him. All I can allow him is, that he may be in the right as well as I, and that we are essentially different in this particular. He may, perhaps, perceive something simple and continu'd which he calls *himself*; tho' I am certain there is no such principle in me.[16]

Edwards remarks that Ramsey attempted to teach a lesson in philosophy to Hume based on Hume's confession that he was puzzled by his feelings of personal identity and driven to skepticism by his not knowing how to correct his former opinions, nor how to render them consistent. Ramsey points out that while actions and behavior do come to our senses as impressions, it is obvious from Hume's quandary that the "feeling" of self or the intuition of self-awareness is based on the "more" or the "I," *the* personal identity which cannot be treated in terms of a narrow empiricism since the "more" "is not a perceptually verifiable 'more.' "[17]

Ramsey's disagreement with Ryle was much more gentle and polite. Edwards suggests that Ramsey felt "inhibited" in criticizing a senior colleague. What concerned Ramsey about the concept of self expressed in Ryle's *The Concept of Mind* was that "Ryle's approach has reduced the observer to what he is observing. . . . We have lost the 'I' which will always elude capture in the scientific net."[18] Later, Ramsey pressed for the "more" in the "I" not considered by Ryle. While accepting Ryle's insistence that the "I" be identified with the awareness of a perception, Ramsey asks whether there might be in some way or another concomitant with each perception an awareness of an invariant factor. Perhaps this invariant factor, observationally elusive, is given in self-awareness and it is this to which "I" refers. Moreover, if this elusive area is witnessed to in a self-referential way by the "I" which always escapes objectification, then this would account for the peculiar logic of the semantics of "I." Ramsey is careful to note, however, that he is not making a case for some kind of metaphysical or transcendental ego which inhabits a different realm and which as somehow untouched by space and time is beyond any meaningful validation. He admits that his recommendation

at this point is very modest and negative. He suggests that
the "I" he speaks of does indeed refer to a fact—though an
elusive one—and that this fact cannot be placed logically in
spatio-temporal language.[19]

Ramsey turned to George Berkeley for support for the notion
that some words function meaningfully in spite of the fact
that they did not correspond to sense impressions. One of these
words is "I," which Ramsey admitted to be "systematically
elusive." Following Berkeley's lead, Ramsey contended that
while "I" is not empirically descriptive, publicly observable
or philosophically analyzable, yet it is certainly significant in
its "wider" or "broader" use. The meaning of "I" in and
from which the "more" may be discerned stems from the development of a pattern from the discrete actions and events of
life, but also from an extended pattern of activity—a gestalt.
Thus, according to Ramsey, we become aware of ourselves
through a disclosure that fashions for our awareness a synthetic
unity for the train of perceptions that comprise our past. The
"I" which is so disclosed is, no doubt, comprised of observable
and scientifically explicable parts; but it is more than all its
parts, more than the sum of the "distinct perceptions" in terms
of which David Hume described experience.[20]

Thus, for Ramsey, "I" is not events or facts alone, yet they
are necessary foundations for the disclosure of self-identity
or self-understanding. Who "I am" is "more than descriptive
discourse can answer." Still Ramsey does develop a more definitive explanation of personality. Rather than conceiving the personality in static or substantive terms, Ramsey urges that we
regard the self as a process. Accordingly, the personality is
identified with a distinctive kind of activity which is owned,
localized and individual in character. The unity of personality
is to be found in an ongoing integrating activity. While it is
always possible to describe scientifically the genetic, biochemi-
cal, endocrinal, electronic, neurological and psychological manifestations of personality's embodiment, the peculiarly human
integrating activity which gives rise to personal existence is

that "more" which escapes the net of the categories of natural science.[21]

Ramsey also was very much aware that many questions still remained about his notion of the "more." In fact, in his article, "Possibility and Purpose of Metaphysical Theology," he asks rhetorically," . . . where the 'more' cannot be perceptually verified . . . what is its empirical basis? How do we come to recognize this 'more'?" And he answers that although the "more" is beyond perceptual verification it is nevertheless recognizable in terms of experience. Ramsey employs the biblical story in which the prophet Nathan's tale of the poor shepherd and his rich neighbor dramatically discloses to David his past pattern of behavior as adulterous and murderous. This story, for Ramsey, illustrates the way the disclosure of the "I" refers to more than what could be observed by anyone else or could be *a-fortiori* described in terms of discrete observable facts. Ramsey goes on to note how this term, "I," though not itself descriptive, can be united with any number of descriptive words. Thus we say, "I am angry," "I am a malaria case," "I am neurotic," "I am a wage earner," and so on. In all of these descriptive statements, the claim "I exist" is presupposed. This presupposed "I" appears to function as an integrator for all the statements in which the "I" occurs in connection with such logically diverse conceptual matrices as those of economics, psychology, or medicine. The "I" of "I exist," discerned as more than what is spatially and temporally observable, is best regarded as a genuinely meaningful metaphysical notion. While not strictly reducible to any objectifiable experience, the "I" as a metaphysical integrator of various domains of objective experience makes possible the unity of human experience and understanding.[22]

Thus for Ramsey, the "more" possesses objectivity on two counts: first, it is anchored in experience, for as Ramsey insists, "all experience is *of* something," and second, it itself is a reality, an activator of disclosure which is a response to and thus the "more" of external experience. The "more" of "I" is quite real and objective. Ramsey never put it more sharply than in his paper in *Personality and Science.*

> Let us argue by a *reductio ad absurdum.* Suppose nothing more were to be said about human beings. Then each human being would be a set—admittedly very complex—of discriminated observables, scientific objects, discerned behaviour patterns, a set of these and no more. This may seem not at all implausible about everybody—except ourselves. As an account by ourselves of ourselves it would clearly be a logical blunder. For any of us to talk of a group of *objects* presupposes a correlative *subject.* Whatever is observed implies an observer who is a presupposition of the resultant discourse and cannot be netted within it.[23]

Later in *Christian Discourse,* Ramsey amplifies his concept of "objectivity" (of the "more" as well as disclosures). Herein he emphasizes that the "more" of a disclosure is "objective" in the sense that it challenges or confronts us in a way that implies a reality other than a mere emanation of ourselves. The objectivity of the "more" which is disclosed is then not like the objectivity of dream images. But neither, according to Ramsey, is the "more" anything like the objectivity which belongs to physical objects or scientific causes. If anything at all, the objectivity of the "more" is experienced as most akin to the way other persons confront us, or the way we intuitively feel the absolute claim of duty.[24] We will return to the subject of disclosures later in the chapter, but it must be noted here that a disclosure of the "more" occurs when an external agency confronts our experience and by that activity reveals the "more" in the situation. Such an encounter is obvious in personal situations, but Ramsey also insists that such activity is present in moral claims as well as in our response to an aesthetic situation. Ramsey notes that moral claims "may be . . . compared with the claims another person makes on us in social behavior,"[25] and that "something is exhibited which is characteristically personal"[26] in our response to a disclosure of beauty.

Ramsey suggests that the analogy of personal activity in disclosure also extends to those situations resulting from concrete particulars and scientific models, in that objects and attendant concepts initiate some personal response. Indeed, he remarks that "personal models will always have a central place in any adequate discourse—even scientific—about the Universe."[27] Thus, Ramsey argues that the insights which are the building blocks of scientific induction are disclosures in a sense akin to the disclosure of the "I." Indeed, according to Ramsey, it is these disclosures which make possible reliable discourse about the phenomena of natural science. Later in *Models and Mystery* he adds, ". . . models in science not only enable us to generate verifiable deductions, and models in theology not only make possible empirical fit. They [also] arise out of, and in this way become currency for a universe that discloses itself to us in a moment of insight."[28] And in his "Reply" to several reviews of *Models and Mystery* Ramsey insists, "My point is that science can only claim to talk of the Universe if the reference of the facts and features verified by its discourse is disclosure given."[29]

Ramsey also illustrates the experience of discernment—insight—disclosure which occurs in a somewhat analogous way to that of personal activity by reference to both mathematical and gestalt insights when something "more" is disclosed. For instance, in a mathematical procedure involving succession of fractions toward "infinite sum" the next full digit is disclosed and the "light dawns."[30] Or when "the penny drops" in gestalt psychology and the whole is discerned as more than the sum of its parts.[31]

C. Words about God: Meaning and Sense
in Religious Language

1. Ramsey's Disclosure Theory: Discernment and Commitment

In the preceding paragraphs, we have examined Ramsey's attempt to define the notions of disclosure and discernment in such a way as to satisfy both analytic philosophy's demand for anchoring religious discourse in experience and religious faith's assertion of the reality of the transcendent or supernatural. It is because Ramsey's notions of discernment and disclosure serve such a function of bridging the epistemological interests of analytic philosophy's methodological commitments and religious belief's ontological commitments that these concepts play such a crucial role in his apologetic for Christian belief. Given the pivotal role these notions play in Ramsey's apologetic account of religious language, they merit an even more detailed exposition.

Ramsey designates the quintessential disclosure of religious experience a "cosmic disclosure." As indicated earlier, a cosmic disclosure arises from situations in which the empirical is extended beyond the ordinary, observable facts and the "more" is disclosed as a special dimension which cannot be explained by sense experience. Ramsey says that "Such a discernment lies at the basis of religion, whose characteristic claim is that there are situations which are spatio-temporal and 'more.' "[32] Thus, for Ramsey, disclosure begins with an empirical situation and moves to an evocation of discernment when "the penny drops," "the ice breaks," "the light dawns" and the situation "comes alive" to draw forth a personal response of commitment.

Actually, Ramsey gives no precise definition of discernment; however, he does offer many illustrations showing it to be that which accompanies disclosure of the empirical and "more." He also shows that science makes use of disclosures-discernments in generalizations, hypotheses and laws. He says, "the scientist . . . does not keep all that close to 'the facts.' What he needs besides and more than the facts, is insight, intuition, some sort of disclosure."[33] Another interesting illustration Ramsey gives of a disclosure-discernment is that perceptual experience in which what first appears as one-dimensional lines drawn on a flat surface are subsequently, in a flash as it were, seen as a three-dimensional cube. Twelve straight lines may appear at first sight as no more than two squares with their corners joined. However, as we continue to look, there "dawns" on us "depth" and the twelve straight lines now appear as a unity. We now see a cube and the lines now are seen in such a way that they seem to enter into or stand out of the surface on which they are drawn. Clearly a new situation, at a definitely recognizable point, has dawned on us. The twelve straight lines have ceased being merely twelve straight lines, and now, from the point of view of plane geometry, odd words like "depth," "volume," or a "new dimension," are required to describe this characteristically different situation.[34]

While considering Ramsey's discussion of the disclosures inherent in self-awareness, we have already seen one of Ramsey's examples of a disclosure coming from moral discernment, that of David who comes to himself with Nathan's challenge, "Thou art the man." Indeed, his many examples of moral discernment[35] are all grounded in situations, yet the ethical judgments which the situations elicit result from the transcending aspects of duty and demand which are disclosed or discerned.

Ramsey, however, does explain the special sense in which a disclosure is religious. Like every disclosure, that which is discerned in religious experience possesses the objectivity of something which confronts or challenges us. In the case of religious disclosure, the universe in its totality is manifested through some group of events in a particular way. Thus the content of the religious disclosure exhibits a cosmic significance.[36]

Ramsey's concept of commitment, while no more precisely defined than disclosure-discernment, seems understandable and not too far from ordinary usage in its significance. For Ramsey, commitment is the appropriate response to what is discerned in every disclosure which "combines the 'depth' of personal or quasi-personal loyalty . . . with the range of mathematical and scientific devotion."[37] It is quite obvious that Ramsey believes that both discernment and commitment are in some sense a necessary combination for the setting in which religious lan-

guage becomes meaningful. In *Religious Language* he argues
that

> Butler suggests that religion claims (a) a fuller discernment, to which
> we respond with (b) a total commitment. Such a commitment without
> any discernment whatever is bigotry and idolatry; to have the discernment
> without an appropriate commitment is the worst of all religious vices.
> It is insincerity and hypocrisy.[38]

Thus Ramsey identifies religious language as expressing a combination of what we "see" (discernment) and "feel" (commitment). And since ordinary language arising from moral or social
experiences often expresses a similar combination of discernment and commitment, religious language exhibits an essential
continuity with linguistic responses we make to ordinary situations at various levels of human experience. It is this fact,
according to Ramsey, which is "the main point" of his empiricist account of religious language. Yet Ramsey admits that
religious situations are often so complex that it is necessary
to "preserve a faithful understanding of its own mysterious
topic."[39] Because of this double characterization of discernment
and commitment Ramsey concludes,

> . . . that for the religious man "God" is a key word, an irreducible
> posit, an ultimate of explanation expressive of the kind of *commitment*
> he professes. It is to be talked about in terms of the object-language
> over which it presides, but only when this object-language is qualified;
> in which case this qualified object-language becomes also currency for
> that odd *discernment* with which religious *commitment*, when it is not
> bigotry or fanaticism, will necessarily be associated.[40]

Ramsey gives many illustrations of his notion of disclosure-
discernment-commitment. Actually the bulk of his writing is
a conscious endeavor to illuminate and explicate his theory
of religious language. We find the same theme even in his
classroom lectures on "miracles," wherein he insists that a
miracle is an event in the experience of man which does not
conform to any scientific explanation, but which is in itself a

cosmic disclosure of such power that "we use the language of personal decisive activity" in speaking about it. Calling miracles "God's activity," therefore, enables him to refer to the Resurrection as "the one theological expression of the Christian's claim for a uniquely decisive activity of God in Jesus Christ."[41] In a paper entitled "The Logical Character of Resurrection-belief," Ramsey shows "that belief in the resurrection is *something more* than belief in a matter of fact."[42] He uses the story of Christ's disciple, Thomas, who after discerning his risen Master in a cosmic disclosure responds with the greatest Christian commitment, "My Lord and my God." Thus we observe that religious commitment offered in response to the discernment of the "more" in cosmic disclosures is as Ramsey put it, "a *total* commitment to the *whole* universe . . . the cosmic Christ of Ephesians and Colossians."[43] And he notes in "A Personal God" that many of us can recall occasions when the Universe has suddenly manifested itself in this lively, personal way.

The main explicatory thesis in Ramsey's philosophy of religion is his analogy of I (as the "more" of human behavior) and God (as the "more" of the Universe). He holds that just as knowledge of self involves a disclosure which goes beyond observable behavior, so knowledge of God involves a cosmic disclosure of the whole universe which goes beyond the spatio-temporal. And as we have seen, while both kinds of knowledge are grounded in a situation of facts and observables, and include the temporal, yet both transcend the situation and lead to such disclosures as make us "aware of an *activity* confronting, engaging our own . . . [which] we may call God."[44] Further, Ramsey argues elsewhere that we can be "as certain of God as we are of ourselves. . . . But no description is guaranteed (of God or self). The basic assertion about God does not stand or fall on one or many particular verifiable assertions. Yet as with ourselves so with God, intuition and description come together."[45] Thus for Ramsey both I and God transcend description; while they are both disclosed through observables, "united

with verifiably descriptive words, without themselves being verifiably descriptive."[46]

Evans indicates that Ramsey supports his analogy by reference to the special loving, personal activity of Jesus Christ,
whom Evans calls the "most" of God's self-disclosure, as well
as by reference to the special behavior of Christians and the
church in their total commitment of worship and witness to
the divine disclosure. Evans notes that for Ramsey, the love
disclosed in Jesus Christ is such a unique disclosure that Christians have responded in such a way that both "can be for
other men an occasion for cosmic disclosure."[47]

In summary, then, it seems clear that for Ramsey religious
disclosures (religious discernments to which we make religious
commitments) are of the utmost importance in explaining his
theory of religious language. Indeed, they may be said to be
both the referent and source of the religious language which
strives to represent and express the "more," or what Ramsey
also calls "the cosmic dimension." Thus the phenomenon we
call religious experience is defined as the discernment of a
cosmic disclosure developed through ordinary experience of
the divine "more" and the response of personal commitment:
and thereby believers claim to have experienced an awareness
of God. However, he does make a sharp distinction between
subjective and objective experience holding that God is always
the discloser and never an object. In making this distinction
he is very close to Paul Tillich and John A. T. Robinson.
Yet, in spite of the importance to religious language of Ramsey's
notions of disclosure-discernment-commitment, religious language can only report these phenomena, says Ramsey, by means
of qualified models.

2. Ramsey's Theory of Qualified Models and Its Function in Religious Language

Many have called Ramsey's theory of models (qualified in
specific ways) his greatest contribution to the philosophy of

religion or, more specifically, to "words about God." Others, notably Braithwaite and Joan Miller, have been very critical of his theory. But he did successfully challenge both the traditional and logical-empirical wings to get at the heart of the problem of words about God, i.e., Is anthropomorphism (reference to God in human terms) really talk about man and not God? Ramsey asks, "If we are not to use anthropomorphic concepts like love, power, wisdom, we cannot talk about God; but if we *do* use them, how do we manage to talk of God and not man?"[48] He answers by showing that words about God can be meaningful in spite of the limitations on religious language proposed by Flew and others. To Flew he points out that while "God is a loving father" is not a pictorial model and is somewhat problematical, yet we may still "decide *which* development inferences are *reliable*" within "the problem which arises when a loving father by himself evokes a cosmic disclosure."[49] And he chides Flew by pointing out that his method of models and metaphors in religious language does not bring " 'death by a thousand qualifications.' Rather is it life by a thousand enrichments."[50]

But what are these qualified models which are so important for Ramsey's theory of religious language? First, let us consider the meaning and function of models. A model Ramsey defined as "a situation with which we are all familiar, and which can be used for reaching another situation with which we are not so familiar; one which, without the model, we should not recognize so easily."[51] Ramsey credits Max Black for his development of the notion in *Models and Metaphors*,[52] but adds to Black's "picture model" (a scale model of the original) his "disclosure model" (an abstract reproduction or representation of the original) as a tool to guide us in understanding religious language. Ved Mehta quotes Ramsey's summary-definition of a model as "any kind of picture or example on which people can agree and by which they can be led to understand something of which at present they are not certain or about which they are perplexed."[53] And Ramsey insists that far more of ordinary language than we realize is characterized by this feature. Thus models can be said to be the observable dimension in the situation that is the foundation for religious disclosure. And they can be ethical (good), philosophical (being), scientific (cause), or metaphorical (father) in nature. Ramsey, of course, emphasized disclosure models since they are "rooted in disclosures and born in insight,"[54] and thus have the power to evoke new disclosures in science as well as all other fields. He stated, "It is my thesis, then, that by virtue of the models they variously incorporate or the metaphors which they employ, or the distinctions native to their exercise, all disciplines combine insight and discursive reasoning, mystery as well as understanding."[55] Yet, while including theology in the above, Ramsey does point out that the emphasis in theology is more on the insight and the mystery and less on reasoning and understanding; and truth depends upon the test of empirical fit rather than deductive verifications.

Qualifiers are an equally important (some say the most important) element in Ramsey's theory of religious language. A qualifier Ramsey defined as "a directive which prescribes a special way of developing . . . model situations"[56] toward a cosmic disclosure or which calls attention to the disclosure-situation and the dimension which is "more" than the empirical factors. Such words are prescriptive in nature and are intended to reveal the "original" the models represent which cannot be pictured or described completely, but which can be disclosed. They are the nonobservable dimensions (conceptual and spiritual) which move a model in a certain way, disclosing the divine dimension in the situation. Ramsey's qualifiers are mostly drawn from Christian theology and are used to overcome the "temptation" in religious language to rely on one model alone. According to Ramsey, these qualifiers serve as a built-in stimulus for the never-ending development of any theological model. These qualifiers, operating as symbols, will suggest an endless series of various revelations of God and when these symbols are paired with one another they will convey other implicitly metaphorical manifestations of the Divine reality. All of these qualified models will point to a cosmic disclosure as that which uniquely reveals the topic of any possible theological utterance. Thus, qualifiers perform a double duty; they witness to the special logical claim of words about God by their ability to multiply models without end, e.g., infinite, and they function as a device to prompt or evoke awareness by means of stories connected with models, e.g., all-loving.

Evans has called attention to Ramsey's three major uses of qualifiers: universalizing (all-mighty); perfecting (perfection); and negating (immutable). Most of the traditional attributes ascribed to God come under the heading of "universalizing," and mostly in two-word combinations with qualifiers, like the *all* in almighty, *first* cause, and *eternal* purpose, which reveal both the empirical grounding and the logical oddness of religious language. The words *mighty*, *cause* and *purpose* are models and the words *all*, *first* and *eternal* are the qualifiers which indicate the way the models are to be developed (to the highest degree beyond observables). Such a task sometimes calls for an "analogical" pointer, e.g., the use of the familiar qualifier "first" to point to an inferred similarity beyond experience. They also reveal the logical limitations of a model term applied to God, e.g., infinitely "perfecting," words which generate perfection, e.g., *infinitely* and *perfect*, and which describe God by contrast. Ramsey suggests that the model "good" is developed (like perfection) by analyzing imperfect human experiences in a hierarchy of decreasing imperfection, and finally by accepting an "odd" or unique discernment we know the new term and its meaning. In describing the theoretical project of transforming a polygon into a circle in terms of an operation that would infinitely increase the number of sides of a polygon whose area remained constant, Ramsey provides an analogy to the way the term "infinite" is used to qualify the notion of God. In the case of the polygon, no matter how many sides have been specified, the term "infinite" tells us not to stop, but to construct a regular polygon with at least one more side.

This succession of constructions could go on indefinitely, but at some point the outline of something quite different, namely a circle, would be manifest. Then, at this point, what could be called a "mathematical insight" would be evoked. The way in which the circle's nature is disclosed—through the construction of a polygon that is qualified as virtually infinite—illumines the way in which the term "infinite" qualified "God." Just as it is difficult to talk of a polygon with an infinite number of sides and just as the word "circle" is nothing if not incommensurate with the "straight-line" language of polygons, so it is difficult to talk about anything we experience as perpetually surpassing any imagined limit and the word "God" is nothing if not incommensurate with the language of finitude.[57]

The third type of qualifiers Evans names as "negating," words which express the negative attributes or characteristics of God with the use of the qualifier "not," such as "immutable" or "impassible." The function of these negating qualifiers is to evoke in us the insight that God is "not," for example, anything mutable or passible. Thus to speak of God as immutable or impassible is to refer to a characteristically different situation than anything we can perceive. The negative words, in a way, make a language plea. They point to a meaning for the word "God" that is beyond all language about the mutable and passible. However, it would be a mistake to find in such a negative theology anything more than the disclaimer about the adequacy of all our language of the passible and mutable in reference to God. The primary value then of such attribute words like impassible and immutable is to evoke in us the discernment which is the basis for talking about God.[58]

Evans also compares negating qualifiers with both perfecting and universalizing qualifiers beyond the obvious denial of negating attributes and the affirmation of perfect and universal attributes. For one thing, negating qualifiers exclude everything observable and the "more," while universalizing and perfecting qualifiers include both the observables and the "more" in relation to what is disclosed.

Evans further shows that models for God may qualify each other, e.g., "father" and "strong tower," which he calls "a haphazard piling up of models." Yet Ramsey does not consider this as a fault; indeed he says that by this is the mystery

safeguarded . . . by qualifying [a model] with other models in a single discourse. . . . by recognizing that to talk adequately of the God who is disclosed on any occasion will need language called from and growing out of all the models which arise in all the vast variety of circumstances God has been disclosed. So Jesus is spoken of as shepherd, prophet, priest, my husband, friend, and king. In this kind of way, we see piling up of models, each qualifying the next.[59]

Ramsey then goes on to advise us on the use of qualified models. First, he insists that, while religious statements are in part descriptive, "Qualifiers have to be added if they are going to take us to God, if they are to prepare us for a disclosure. . . . 'God is loving,' 'God exists,' are . . . logically incomplete . . . so that we more aptly say that God is infinitely loving, God necessarily exists."[60] Second, he argues that, while models do provide the content of religious utterances, they "never exhaust the mystery" and "provide only partial understanding" so that "inferences from those models become precarious" causing us to ever "look for more . . . adequate models for talking about that mystery which is God."[61] Indeed, we may also use a variety of models with multiple-word qualifiers, a usage we have discussed above. Third, Ramsey adds that what he develops in the model-qualifier disclosure leading to a response of personal commitment involves "what might be called . . . a logical leap . . . like [that of] Kierkegaard. . . . But for me . . . it can be pictured . . . as a leap into the arms of a loving Father. . . ."[62] So, for Ramsey, the "leap" is not across a "grim broad chasm," but is a "being carried over," a continuous process within human experience made possible within the mystery which is God.

For Ramsey, qualified models will be disclosure models representing phenomena, yet are always "more" than the facts of the situation as these qualified models are evoked in the disclosure. Thus, all theological models are cosmic (unlimited, extra spatio-temporal) disclosures which emphasize mystery and transcendence. As he says in *On Being Sure in Religion,* qualified models "are of use when they are acceptable, persuasive, clear and so reliable guides to what at the present baffles us . . . to evoke a disclosure— . . . —*to bring us to God.*"[63] Tilley notes five uses or functions of qualified models: (1) to refer to the "more" (God) encountered in a cosmic disclosure; (2) to represent this special "more" through everyday language; (3) to indicate by the use of qualifiers that the "more" (God) stands outside of everyday language, though related to it in a continuum; (4) to evoke disclosures, inasmuch as a successful pattern of qualified models will always lead to religious discernment and commitment (of and to God); (5) to generate stories and license discourse of the person and acts of God. Of course such stories and discourse must lead us to God, otherwise such language is misleading or deceptive.

In *Religious Language,* Ramsey summarizes his discussion of the logical behavior of qualified models as disclosure prompters, noting that we cannot guarantee completely whether any particular model will indeed elicit a disclosure for some individual or group of people. However, we need to recognize that some other stories or qualified models may succeed where the first model failed. For some, disclosure will occur through their hearing causal stories. For others it will be wisdom stories or creation stories, or stories about good lives that bring about religious insight. In fact, notes Ramsey, there is no word which in principle might not be the occasion for evoking the disclosure situation in which God is known. In other words, God may be disclosed in principle at any point within his creation.[64]

Ramsey then illustrates his point by an examination of the traditional problem of evil in the light of his thesis that any word may be a model by means of which a characteristically religious situation can be evoked. First, he analyzed the more traditional theodices, e.g., the unified and descriptive "Fall" theory, the similarly unified and descriptive "permitting" (as opposed to "willing") theory, and a "super-model" theory of evil as God's purposive and redemptive love. Ramsey sees value in them when they are combined in a multi-model discourse, each qualifying the other. Still he insists that we must not forget that our discourse as comprised of models is always a kind of analogical discourse and should never be taken as providing an objective description of the nature of God. The discourse of philosophical theology and Christian doctrine gives us guidelines for consistent talking about the human experience of God. In the case of a theodicy, the language directs us as to how to reckon at the same time with the presence of evil in the universe and its subjection to God. And, according to Ramsey, whatever the model which addresses the problem of evil is, it always does so referring the believer to the empirical situations of "wonder" and "worship."[65] Second, Ramsey's reply to J. L. Mackie's paper, "Evil and Omnipotence," which he entitled "The Paradox of Omnipotence," illustrates the application of his model-qualifier pattern. He argues that the logic of omnipotence is not what Mackie suggests, but that "potent" is a familiar, empirical model with "omni" the logically odd qualifier. It is in their combination that we move somewhat closer to the understanding of the nature of God in the face of evil, with language indicating not a paradox, but a special logical pattern evoking a disclosure with reference to a characteristically religious situation—one of worship, wonder and awe.

Ramsey discusses a goodly number of examples of his analysis and method in Chapters III and IV of *Religious Language,* "The Language of the Bible" and "The Language of Christian Doctrine." As a general principle, Ramsey notes that biblical language more directly prompts disclosure and commitment, while theological language relies more heavily on the model-qualifier pattern. His "general reflections" on biblical literature are interesting and his conclusions helpful.

1. No attempt to make the language of the Bible conform to a precise straightforward public language—whether that language be scientific or historical—has ever succeeded.

2. More positively, the Bible is about situations as odd as those which
we have had in mind throughout this book; the kind of situation to
which existentialists refer when they speak of something being "authentic" or "existential-historical." The "facts" of the Gospels in
particular are never facts for which science is appropriate currency,
or history is appropriate currency.[66]

One interesting example taken from the Old Testament and
developed by Ramsey is the Jewish reticence in naming God,
which he sees as an effort to preserve the spiritual dimension
of religious or cosmic disclosure. Indeed, Ramsey notes that
in those biblical episodes which apparently record God disclosing his name, what in fact occurs is a characteristically religious
situation with language appropriate to such a situation. Our
customary notion of a name then does not accurately reflect
the disclosure-situation conveyed by the biblical episodes associated with the declaration of God's various names. This can
be seen quite clearly, Ramsey points out, in the Exodus 3
story wherein God's declared name, "I am that I am" discloses
to Moses the full commitment and trust required on his part
in response to God's call.[67]

A parallel example in the New Testament is the manifold
and varied names and titles accorded to Jesus Christ. In *Religious Language*, Ramsey discusses "Son of Man" primarily,
although elsewhere[68] he considers many more including "Mes-
siah" and "High Priest." He notes the logical address of "Son
of Man" and shows it to be both descriptive (who Jesus was)
and evocative (relates Jesus to God and to the redeeming nature
of Israel). In his article which first appeared in *The Chicago
Theological Seminary Register*, he wrote, ". . . my contention
is that the most significant titles of Jesus are those which incorporate and provide models which are grounded in a disclosure,
on the one hand, and enable us to be reliably articulate about
the Gospel, on the other."[69]

In presenting examples from theological language, Ramsey
offers his own set of models necessary to ground Christian
doctrines in human experience and the qualifiers necessary

to maintain both the logical uniqueness and the special dimension of such belief. "Son of God" is a doctrine in point. The model "Son" is qualified usually by such a term as "only" in order to preserve an empirical anchor and provide for the necessary logical uniqueness to thwart heresy. Ramsey explained this maneuver in *Religious Language:*

> As we survey the developments of Christology and Trinitarian doctrine, what is evident, however, is how often the heretics run some model or other—sometimes a highly sophisticated model—to death, in a passionate desire to understand. Opponents then come forward with other models which show the inadequacy of the first, but they too develop them beyond necessity, and court fresh heresies at the next move. But let us not be made sceptical by such shuttlecock theology . . . of the early history of Christian doctrine which only arises because the ball could never be left to rest in any one empirical court. The struggle to understand God can never come to a satisfactory end; the language game can never be completed. Broadly speaking, what orthodoxy did was to support the winner of every heat.[70]

Further, Ramsey notes that:

> What the early controversies settled were . . . rules for our talking, and what came out of them at the end were new symbols for our use, and in particular the Trinitarian formula. The Christian does not have the single word "God" as his key word. He substitutes for that symbol another; and this other symbol is built out from that focus of our total commitment which is made up of the elements of the Christian dispensation . . .
> The Christian says in effect—for "God" read
> Father
> Son—Holy Spirit.[71]

And referring to the Athanasian Creed, Ramsey concludes that what it does specifically

> . . . is to commend as the Christian key word a new symbol for "God." It formulates rules for its construction; it gives the symbol an appropriate logical structure. For the most part the Creed is thus purely formal, and needs for its understanding and content the Christian disclosure which, at best, would be otherwise given in that worshipful situation where the Creed naturally occurs.[72]

In another place, Ramsey also shows how the doctrine of
the Trinity harmonizes the empirical facts of biblical history—
the Person of Jesus Christ and the testimony and life of the
early church—with theological mystery. He points out that
when these elements are considered as qualified models, e.g.,
"The Father uncreated, incomprehensible . . . eternal," they
work from situations with which we are familiar through language signposts to the odd logical placing of our key word
"God." In his paper, "A Logical Exploration of Some Christian
Doctrines," he summarizes his basic position first by quoting
Hilary of Portiers, "We must therefore regard any comparison
[between God and earthly things] as helpful to man rather
than as descriptive of God, since it suggests rather than exhausts
the sense we seek. . . . Neither speech of man nor the analogy
of human nature can give us full insight into the things of
God. . . . We must understand Him [God] by devotion and
confess Him by reverence."[73] Second, he then concludes that:
"What is quite plain is that the Trinity is not concerned to
report on God's private life; it does not describe what goes
on in the Godhead, it is no descriptive blueprint of God. The
Doctrine of the Trinity is rather something which offers us
complex logical guidance to talk about a mystery."[74] Thus Ramsey shows that doctrines examined by his method of qualified
models evoking disclosure is helpful to man in his understanding of divine mystery rather than a straightforward description
of God suggesting rather than exhausting its theme. In this
insight we go beyond Max Black's original thesis and see the
implications for theology, when theology is construed as a
purveyor of disclosure, a discipline which calls attention to
those qualifiers which will be associated with models so as to
make religious language meaningful and helpful.

3. Ramsey's Case for the Metaphysical in Empirical Theology

Ramsey has demonstrated the significance of qualified models
in making logical mapping of religious language possible by

providing a pattern within the situations and a conceptual framework without which religious disclosure would be impossible. Indeed, for him, religious language is a disclosure model with "God" as its key word, the special word for the experience and the expression of the unobservable, an integrator word to help determine our "cosmic position" and thus the "cosmic mapping" of both language and belief. And while religious language is in constant contact with the empirical and is explicable in terms of ordinary language, its main function is metaphysical: to provide linguistic integration necessary to express the nonobservable transcending the spatio-temporal facts and science. Indeed, Ramsey describes the function of disclosure models as: "to point to and to hint at a further dimension, and it will do this primarily by its qualifiers which like a 3-D viewer bring diverse pictures together until they witness to the 'depth' which each alone misses and conceals."[75]

It was Ramsey's announced intention to join in what G. J. Warnock, writing in *English Philosophy Since 1900*, noted as recent attempts to make metaphysics more meaningful in terms of a "fresh light," of "ways of seeing," or of "disclosures" which produce "alternative conceptual systems."[76] Ramsey hoped to present an empirically based metaphysical system coherent with both science and analytic philosophy. In his preface to *Religious Language*, subtitled with the challenging Welsh phrase, *Cydnabyddraeth a Chyffes* (knowledge which excites), he encouraged his philosophical and theological colleagues and critics to "look sometime in another book which I hope soon to publish under the title of *Fact, Metaphysics and God.*"[77] Unfortunately the book was never completed. Yet we may take some consolation from Ramsey's contribution to a book which he edited, *Prospect for Metaphysics*, in which he does provide an insight into his special conviction that metaphysics has a place in the "doing" of philosophical theology.

In "On the Possibility and Purpose of a Metaphysical Theology" (chastened by logical empiricism), Ramsey made a case for a reconstructed metaphysics based on C. D. Broad's phrase, "critical common sense." According to Ramsey, "it would be concerned, in a critical fashion, to organize common-sense assertions in accordance with some perspective or other." He insisted that "metaphysics is no mere extension of ordinary language" and reminds us of Butler's pregnant reminder, "Everything is what it is, and not another thing." Thus, his conclusion is that descriptive metaphysics is empiricism "and more," a conclusion which he noted was supported by many of his peers who were participating in the broadening of empiricism, namely, Wittgenstein, Strawson, and Hare.

In sum, Ramsey writes

> . . . metaphysics, to be genuine metaphysics, must have reference to more than observables, i.e., to the unseen. If our reasoning is reliable, this is in fact our conclusion. For metaphysical integrators, being not native to any scientific language, must have their grounding in what is more than spatio-temporal, i.e., they must be "meta-physical" in a more obviously traditional sense. For metaphysics is not merely . . . the construction of some kind of ancillary map—it is . . . the construction of a map in accordance with a vision of the unseen.[78]

Thus he returns to his original claim that while metaphysical theology is no mere extension of ordinary language, yet, like scientific language, it is related to it. Ramsey's notion of the "more" supplies his support for metaphysical language, which, like scientific language, has its foundation in empirical observables, yet also possesses a dimension which goes beyond and is not reducible to those observables. And again he turns to his keystone doctrine, the unique logic of self-knowledge and the linguistic use of "I." Ramsey insists that the situation which justifies metaphysics is the same as that which justifies our own use of "I," and in this word "I" we have a paradigm for all metaphysical integrators.

Further, exploring the "more" in the model "I" and its empirical basis, Ramsey answers the question, How do we come to recognize (verify) this special "more"? He explains his often-used story of David and Nathan:

Notice the technique. Nathan tells David a story which David understands—as a spectator—in terms of "objects." There are two men, the one rich, the other poor. The rich man had many flocks and herds, the poor man had nothing, except one little ewe lamb. Unexpected visitors arrive, and the rich man's wife is "on the spot." She spares to take of her husband's flock, for whatever reason we can only invent, and sends to the poor man for his little lamb, etc.—a story perfectly coined in terms of objects. David understands it—he builds up the object picture, and he makes an impersonal judgement on it as though he were Mr. Justice David sitting in the Queen's Bench division. "That man must surely die." Here is something all very impersonal—scientific and legal. But then Nathan challenges David, "Thou art the man," and the penny drops—there is a disclosure indeed. David surveys his distinct perceptions—on the one hand the lamb, the two men, the guests and so on and, alongside this, the picture of Bathsheba and Uriah's death . . . and—he comes to himself. For the first time in that story he has "self-knowledge"; he knows "I."[79]

Needless to say that for Ramsey the unifier and integrator of theism is "God," which Ramsey claims to be the integrator word which provides the most simple, far-reaching and coherent map. He asks how it is we are to understand our use of this integrator word "God." In the first place, Ramsey proposes, we must model "God" on "I." This means, then, in general that whenever we speak about God we must qualify all descriptive language—whether of people, human behavior, or the Universe—so that this language elicits a disclosure. This is best accomplished by either qualifying descriptive language infinitely or negatively. The peculiar logic of discourse about God is, however qualified, most like the discourse concerning "I" in that both "I" and "God" refer to disclosure situations which cannot be captured totally by descriptive language. Moreover, according to Ramsey, in so far as features of the disclosure situation lead us to beyond what is seen and in so far as we discover common objective constituents of all disclosures, then the possibility of a metaphysical theology arises.[80]

Thus, Ramsey concludes that the key word "God" is to be modeled on the term "I"; a term which provides both a dimension of experience and a vision of the "unseen" and makes possible a disclosure situation which will "guarantee God" to us very much as we are "guaranteed" to ourselves. Yet he adds, "the basic assertion about God does not stand or fall on one or many particular verifiable assertions . . . as with, ourselves, so with God, intuition and description come together."[81] Thus has Ramsey developed his case for the metaphysical in empirical theology. He has argued that metaphysicians and theologians alike need "integrator" words or superordinate and synthetic concepts which are not employed within any one of the special sciences. The concepts of metaphysicians and theologians, though, when properly arrived at, are able to make connection with the way objectivity is constituted in each of the sciences and also to supplement the objectivity of individual sciences by disclosing its limits. As for theological and metaphysical discourse itself, its logical patterns may differ from that of the sciences, since here we have to do with a frame of reference or standpoint that is characteristically different than that of any of the sciences. This in part accounts for what Ramsey refers to as the "oddness" of theological and metaphysical words, i.e., these terms will appear strange or disjointed from within the standpoint of any particular paradigm of objectivity which as such defines the limits of a given scientific discipline.[82]

D. Confirmation and Justification: Ramsey's Wider Empiricism and Theories of Religious Language

1. Justification of Ramsey's Christian Empiricism and of the Logical "Oddness" of Religious Language

It is important in view of Ramsey's claim to have developed a metaphysically chastened empiricism and an empirically chastened metaphysics, to examine his explanation and justification of such a claim. Is he an empiricist in any meaningful sense of that word? Ramsey believes that he is in light of several

important standards: first, he insists that all meaningful language must be grounded in and never lose contact entirely
with experience; second, he points out that religious language
is not dissimilar to scientific language; indeed "it interlocks
with all the diverse languages of science to unite them as a
common presupposition"[83] because the personal features of
both religious and scientific situations provide a common
ground; third, he notes that both religious language and scientific language use qualified models to provide generalizations
or "disclosures," and consequently reliable knowledge. Ramsey
does admit that religious language does not provide the precise
kinds of statements which can be as easily verified as scientific
statements, yet he is quick to point out that verification in
religious language is quite possible in the personal mode based
on the functional, logical relationship of the terms "God" and
"I." He shows that such a phenomenon in religious language
is not too unlike the assertions of natural science which "finds
its empirical basis in a cosmic disclosure . . . mediated to
us, through the patterns of the natural world."[84]

The closest Ramsey ever comes to offering a complete and
comprehensive justification is in his Frederick D. Maurice lectures published under the title *On Being Sure in Religion*.
He acknowledges that religion faces a serious crisis in regard
to the nature of religious knowledge and points out that ". . .
even if philosophy no longer flourishes the nonsense veto which
it did in the thirties nevertheless it still presents us with a
challenge—. . . to religious people to elucidate the empirical
anchorage of their religious assertions."[85] Ramsey lauds Maurice's contribution of providing a viable alternative on the certainty possible in religion and theology, which Ramsey saw
as "to be sure in religion" through the experience of God's
disclosure, but to be "tentative in theology" through the approx-
imations of our language describing the disclosure. Ramsey
also notes a major criterion for the justification of religious
knowledge proposed by Maurice, that of "a broader concept
of reasonableness."[86] Ramsey concludes that religious discern-

ment and commitment, based as they are on disclosure-in-experience, are sure and certifiable, but that theological statements, based as they are on the "odd" logic of qualified models, are approximate and tentative. His support of the first conclusion is the "guarantee" of knowledge supplied in the cosmic disclosure of the coming together of experience and intuition. Thus our knowledge of God, while probable, is certified by the disclosure of God mediated through experience, while our language about God must remain uncertifiable. Still, Ramsey insists that the merit of logical empiricism (used in his way) "is that it provides us with an inroad into theology which can break down misunderstandings, and by centering attention onto both language and 'facts,' can from the beginning hope to be both intellectually honest and devotionally helpful—a combination not always achieved."[87]

Having mentioned the "odd" logic of qualified models in the preceding paragraph, I feel somewhat pressed to examine briefly Ramsey's notion of "logical oddness." While he readily agrees that religious language is appropriately odd and has a distinctive logical behavior in both its insistence on the "more" in empirical situations and on the currency of the strange and unique disclosures coming from and through qualified models, yet Ramsey points out that it is not unlike either ordinary language or some scientific language. Indeed he argues that scientific language has odd aspects (disclosures and the use of qualified models), and following the influence of Wittgenstein, he shows the problematic nature of science and language about natural phenomena which "arise out of, and in this way become currency for, a universe that discloses itself to us in a moment of insight."[88] Ramsey then points out that religious language which deals with the most complex human experiences is bound to exhibit a complex (and thus "odd") logic. He illustrates this with the peculiarities inherent in his analogy of the "I" and "God" and notes that "I" refers both to one's self and to the utterances one makes. Further, Ramsey insists that whatever "oddness" is present is necessary to human discourse about either "I" or "God." Indeed, he holds that regard-less of the field—poetry, science or religion—"there is an im-portant place for odd language; that odd language may well have a distinctive significance, and we might even conclude in the end that the odder the language the more it matters to us."[89]

2. *Criteria for Justification in Ramsey's Theories of Religious Language*

Ramsey has been criticized by some philosophical theolo-gians for neglecting the verification or justification of religious language, e.g., Ninian Smart and Edward Cell, both of whom questioned the cognitive status of Ramsey's theory of disclo-sures and words about God based on qualified models. Several others, however, have pointed out that the criticisms of Smart and Cell, et. al., are based on either a narrow reading of Ramsey or on an oversimplification of his theories. Indeed, Tilley's study on the justification of Ramsey's talk of God shows conclu-sively that Ramsey has a thoroughgoing justificatory theory ranging from an early notion of a situation-based "empirical anchor" to a later notion of "empirical fit."

Ramsey was well aware of the fact that religious language cannot be verified in the way scientific language can. Further, he insisted that theology "cannot and must not provide such verification" since God would then "become a scientific concept."[90] From this theological position, Ramsey developed a metaphysical canon which, according to Tilley, proposed that religious discourse is meaningful if it is consistent, simple, comprehensive or coherent and thus provides a helpful logical mapping of theological language. By *consistent*, Ramsey meant the ability to avoid category mistakes and to sort out a term's (model's) various logical tasks. By *simple* he meant just that, fewer metaphysical words or dominant models—a criterion Ramsey tried to apply in all his explications. By *comprehensive* he meant the subject must be covered but with precision and

interest, yet without irrelevance. By *coherence,* he meant the
integration of terms and language and the elimination of the
self-contradictory and paradoxical. Tilley observes that Ramsey
ranked theism highly as a metaphysics mainly because it is
relatively simple, while also extremely coherent and comprehensive. Yet Tilley further calls attention to the fact that Ramsey
overlooked and underemphasized the first and probably the
most important criterion, consistency.

But the most important general criterion to help us develop
sensible and verifiable religious language is that the term or
model "fit" the empirical situation out of which the term or
model developed. So Ramsey says in *Words About God* that
when Christians speak about the God of love this model of
love can only be justified if there is some pattern of empirical
circumstances which "fit" loving discourse when used of God.[91]
Thus we have Ramsey's material criterion, his theory of "empirical fit." The criterion was first developed in Ramsey's *Models
and Mystery* when he declared, ". . . a theological model is
not judged for its success or failure by reference to the possibility of verifiable deductions. It is rather judged by . . . its
success (or otherwise) in harmonizing whatever events are to
hand." Ramsey then illustrates this testing procedure through
an analogy of a boot fitting the foot and properly serving its
function. He says it is

> . . . more like the fitting of a boot or a shoe than like the "yes" or
> "no" of a roll call. In other words, we have a particular doctrine which,
> like a preferred and selected shoe, starts by appearing to meet our
> empirical needs. But on closer fitting to the phenomena the shoe may
> pinch. When tested against future slush and rain it may be proven to
> be not altogether water-tight or it may be comfortable—yet it must not
> be too comfortable. In this way, the test of a shoe is measured by its
> ability to match a wide range of phenomena, by its overall success in
> meeting a variety of needs. Here is what I might call the method of
> empirical fit which is displayed by theological theorizing. . . .[92]

Later, in answer to his critics of *Models and Mystery,* Ramsey
replied by comparing the theologian as theorist to the archaeol-

ogist or anthropologist or detective who sees how his theory "fits" a particular set of remains—though they may "fit" many other theories, and at certain points fit ill with the one being sponsored.[93] He admitted that theological models are justified in another way from those of science, yet he insisted that there are other ways of justification all of which could be faithful to empirical theology. These other ways may range in various degrees from that of logical fit to a pragmatic, "open-ended" criterion.

Tilley makes a strong case for a pragmatic criterion for the justification of religious language. He notes that Ramsey claimed that philosophy must "culminate in life itself." There is little doubt that Ramsey's notion of commitment included the reflection, in the life of one who has discerned the disclosure of the quality of the truth so discerned. In this he comes very close to Hare's thesis in "Religion and Morals"[94] that how a person behaves is a good way of distinguishing what he or she believes. Indeed, Ramsey admits that in both the quest for disclosure of the good life and the justification of it "the sensitive humanist and the theist have a common quest" for some experiences and attitudes which we call religious. Of course, implicit in the pragmatic criterion are the subtests of consistency (the life lived is consistent with the beliefs claimed) and reliability (the beliefs are comprehensive, coherent and have empirical fit). Tilley sums up Ramsey's use of the pragmatic test. "The whole life of one who believes that God is infinitely loving shows the value of that claim; the whole life of someone who believes that life in the universe is ultimately insignificant shows the value of that claim; the whole life of someone who avoids . . . taking a stand on what matters ultimately shows the value of that stand."[95]

In the face of Ramsey's extensive and unique contributions to philosophical theology, we must conclude that his theories demand a wider reading and a careful examination. Especially is this desirable since Ramsey pioneered the way of offering a (typically Anglican) *via media* between empirical, univocal anthropomorphism on the one hand and metaphysical, analogical mysticism on the other. We also judge that we must examine more fully Ramsey's "Christian empiricism" to determine whether it is in fact an empiricism supporting material analysis or simply an analysis of situations in which religious language is used, which is a formal analysis. Nevertheless, we can be certain that Ramsey always included in his analyses of religious language the factual, the philosophical, the psychological, and the religious factors. In this comprehensiveness he at least covers every important aspect, or as he says in his helpful summary of the "logic of theology" in *Religious Language,* "Theology spends every philosophical model and more." And he concludes, since Christian doctrine does not describe God in the way a verbal photograph, so to speak, might present us with a picture of God, it can only be justified in terms of an epistemology very different from those associated with more traditional metaphysics. The entire focus of Ramsey's notions of "disclosure," the "more," "qualified models," and "discernment" is to make evident that in theology there can be no one-to-one correspondence between religious discourse and that of which it speaks. To believe that such a correspondence is the case in theological assertions would be to confuse the logic of theology with that more precise logic and language that we do employ in the natural sciences.

E. A Summary and a Look Ahead

We have carefully examined Ramsey's claim to be a Christian empiricist and must find in favor of some equivocation on the verdict. Without any question Ramsey did ground religious knowledge and meaningful religious language in experience; yet his empiricism is both "situational," that is, dependent upon an often uniquely singular experience and "wider," which we have come to assess as a something "more" in experience. And we can hardly fault Ramsey's claim that all the classical empiricists as well as many of the later empirical philosophers and theologians tended to offer some notions which broadened the otherwise limited applications of empiricism. We have noted some elements of the empirical in Ramsey's major theories of religious language, i.e., disclosure, qualified models and empirical fit; still we have been well aware of equally important elements of the metaphysical and the mystical which belie the usual criteria of empiricism. However, we did conclude that Ramsey had made a helpful contribution to the meaning and explanatory procedures of theological language in spite of the equivocal status of his empiricism.

In the final chapter we will concern ourselves with the several criticisms mounted against Ramsey's theories of religious knowledge and language. Also we will consider Ramsey's replies in instances where they are in print. Finally, we will weigh these criticisms and replies and conclude with my own personal assessment of Ramsey as a philosophical theologian and churchman.

V. Criticisms, Replies and a Gentle Assessment

A. Introduction

It was inevitable that a theory of religious language and knowledge as unique as that of Ian Ramsey would provoke criticisms from his colleagues in both philosophy and theology. This final chapter will examine many of those criticisms, along with Ramsey's replies where available, and then present what I have called "a gentle assessment" of him as philosopher, theologian and preacher.

B. The Early Critics and Some Replies

1. A. G. M. Flew, in his article, "Can a Man Witness His Own Funeral?"[1], had not mentioned Ramsey at all, but had attacked one of the most important concepts in Ramsey's empirical thesis and explanation of religious language—the meaning of "self" ("I" or "person") which includes the observable and more. Flew concerned himself specifically with the question of what it means to say "We survive death" or "We . . .

live forever." He demonstrated that logically what must be said is, "Nonsense: you either survive or you die!" and empirically, while a man can imagine his own funeral, if it really is his funeral he cannot be a witness, for he shall be dead and in the coffin. Further, Flew points out that to claim immortality from either imagination or from the prescription "Wait until you die!" is both wrong and misleading. He does concede that person words are not synonymous with "body" and that "I" is not a synonym for "my body," nor he insists, is it a synonym for "my mind" or "my soul" or any combination of these. And Flew concludes by reminding us that "Berkeley, with his usual insight remarked, 'the grand mistake is that we know not what we mean by "we," "selves," or "mind," etc.' "[2]

Ramsey promptly replied to Flew in an article, "Persons and Funerals: What Do Person Words Mean?"[3] Ramsey began by giving a clear summary of Flew's arguments: mainly that after death we are no longer alive, and that while a person may be more than his body, "what we are more perishes at death." It is at this point that Ramsey mounts his challenge: "But what in fact do person words mean?" Noting that Flew limits these words to the observable behavior of a "living" body, Ramsey asks if there is something about persons which is "perceptually elusive," something more than behavior which is observable. Using Joseph Butler, from whom Flew had drawn the "strange perplexities" of immortality, Ramsey insists that "we ourselves" are not merely objects, but self-aware, authentic persons. Ramsey also shows that Flew had taken the concluding quotation from Berkeley out of context by giving us the full sentence which concludes: " 'tis most sure and certain that our ideas are distinct from the mind, (i.e.) the will and the spirit."[4] Ramsey also points to David Hume's "feeling of personal identity" as similar to Berkeley's claim of "notions" beyond ideas, calling them odd expressions of personhood which are both elusive and mysterious. Further he claims that such phenomena point to the "more" beyond a person's behavior evoked from

"certain characteristically personal situations." Returning to
Flew's difficulty of witnessing one's own funeral, Ramsey admits
the difficulty but insists that his own funeral will not cover
"all that of which Ramsey is aware when he is aware of himself." It is the *"more"* which will be the subject of philosophical
friends and prompt their "logically appropriate phrases." As
for Ramsey, he "will be content to enjoy 'it' untroubled then
(I hope) by the need to give it a logical mapping."[5] And he
concludes that while death does bring to an end all physical
functions of the body it does *not* bring to an end that something
more which makes persons more than objects and gives person
words their special character.

2. Ramsey's response to R. B. Braithwaite's Eddington Memorial Lecture, "An Empiricist's View of the Nature of Religious Belief," prompted Braithwaite's reply[6] (to Ramsey and
others). Braithwaite had argued in his lecture that religious
assertions are basically moral assertions, and while they are
neither matters of fact (testable by experience) nor matters of
logic (testable as necessary propositions), still they are not meaningless since they declare an ethical attitude and the intention
to act in accordance with that attitude. For example, the statement, "God is love," is a declaration of the Christian to follow
a love-centered way of life. Further, Braithwaite notes that
religious statements are associated with stories, usually with
empirical fit, which are psychologically supportive in the religious man's practice of his moral intentions. Such stories may
or may not be true, nor correspond to empirical fact, yet Braithwaite insists they encourage allegiance to Christian moral principles and the behavior which follows from such commitment.
With such grounding in ethics and human behavior, Braithwaite
believed he had made religious language more meaningful.

The importance of Ramsey's response to Braithwaite's lecture
lies not only in the fact that it defended a more orthodox
account of the Christian's commitment to the moral claim of
God, but also because it introduced many of his major concepts
and dicta. Ramsey criticizes Braithwaite for not recognizing

the "odder" empirical facts of "the religious man's claim for
his religious beliefs to be taken seriously." He points out that
Braithwaite's claim that 1 Corinthians 13 contains "an empirical description" of the agapeistic way of life could lead to
idolatry. Ramsey suggests that the way to empirically discover
the *agape* of 1 Corinthians 13 is to tell a story which begins
with a model situation, using the words of St. Paul, "bearing,"
"believing," "hoping" or "enduring." Then the situation is
developed in a way that the apostle's qualifying phrase "all
things" suggests the story might go on forever. However, Ramsey insists that what happens is that the development of the
empirical situation, based on the models and qualifiers, evokes
a new empirically anchored situation and *agape* is disclosed
to which we respond with an agapeistic way of life.[7] In addition
to presenting his thesis of the meaning of religious language
and introducing his unique terminology, Ramsey also made a
case for the "facts" of Christianity to which the Christian is
committed, which are both biblical and centered in the empirical
Jesus of Nazareth. And he concludes that Christian assertions
declare that "something happened," and while the stories connected with these events are logically odd, they are not fictional.

In his reply to Ramsey, Braithwaite chides him for the unusual use of the words "empirical" and "fact," e.g., in talking
of a Christian declaring a commitment to "facts," a usage which
is a "grave" category mistake (deriving *ought* from *is*). Further,
Braithwaite complained that Ramsey's use of "inverted commas" around "*facts*" and his reference to "odd logic," and
the development of models and qualifiers to gain meaning "will
only save an 'intellectual content' for Christianity at the price
of making it a secret doctrine open only to the Elect."[8]

3. Willem F. Zuurdeeg, a philosophical theologian, announced in his book, *An Analytical Philosophy of Religion*,[9]
a noble purpose of acquainting analytical and empirical philosophers with what can be intelligibly said about religion and
theology. And, like Ramsey, he endeavored to impress theologians with the implications of contemporary philosophy for

their discipline. Further, Zuurdeeg presented his own theory of religious language—that it is convictional, not indicative (matter of fact) nor analytical (matter of logic). Instead, he argued that there are neither scientific proofs nor arguments which can validate or invalidate any conviction since such language is rooted deeply in the person who speaks.

Zuurdeeg rejects "logical analysis" as a fruitful method in philosophy of religion and thus develops an early critique of Ramsey. However, Zuurdeeg admits "that Ramsey is the first theological leader of a Christian church who had done modern analytical philosophers the honor of taking their challenge seriously in order to *think with them* instead of dismissing or ignoring them." What bothers Zuurdeeg the most about Ramsey's method is not its originality nor his germaine questions, e.g., "What is the logical function of the word 'God'?" but the fact that his method does not fit the approach Zuurdeeg developed in terms of convictions. Further, he criticized Ramsey for his characterization of God-talk as logically odd, a negative, artificial "analysis" instead of a positive, convictional life-language. And, Zuurdeeg concluded that while Ramsey was indeed an analytic philosopher of religion, yet the "overall frame" of Ramsey's work is "decidedly convictional" "[and is actually] a theology, an apologetics for a modern form of the Anglican faith."[10]

4. H. D. Lewis in his review of Ramsey's *Freedom and Immortality*,[11] offers what Ramsey calls in his reply[12] "helpful and constructive criticisms" and "sympathetic and generous treatment" of his views. Lewis was a personal friend of Ramsey's, yet his "generous" review was firmly critical. Lewis takes Ramsey to task for not providing the clarity and careful thought he claims on either the concept of freedom or that of immortality. And Lewis observes that Ramsey is less than accurate in his presentation of the case of the libertarians (Where was some explicit reference to C. A. Campbell, an outstanding libertarian?) and less than adequate in his presentation of the Christian case for eternal life. At issue in each instance is Ramsey's central dictum of the "more" in disclosure situations coming

from experience and evoked by qualified models toward "disclosure" of decisions and actions that are free and life that is immortal. Also at issue is Ramsey's concept of the logical kinship between "God" and "I." Lewis argues that the concept is an interesting insight, but notes that Ramsey's references to God as "the objective counterpart to 'I'," etc., are inconclusive as to "what is being affirmed beyond the distinctive characteristics of certain finite situations."[13] Further, Lewis insists that Ramsey was likewise inconclusive about eternal life and chides him that it sounds as though he were saying, "I must have a soul because I am sometimes 'soulful.' " Indeed, as Lewis points out, traditional arguments for immortality insist on both the transcendence of the soul (not "a shadowy existent, some kind of counterpart of the body") and the transcendence of God (not merely a God who is involved in the being of anything).

Ramsey's reply was not entirely reassuring and certainly not a defense against Lewis's carefully argued criticisms. For instance, in answer to Lewis's claim that *God, freedom* and *immortality* are used by Ramsey in such a way that he moves too easily from one to the other, Ramsey counters, that "since the paradigm for understanding all disclosures is the disclosure that each of us has of himself in decisive, free, moral action, our certainty about God is at least like the certainty we have of our own existence."[14] And Ramsey does undertake to answer Lewis's questions as to just what is being affirmed in disclosures beyond the empirical situation. In other words what is the objective referent of Ramsey's disclosure, is it the Christian's transcendent God? Ramsey reiterates his oft-repeated assurance that the empirical grounding of his disclosures is more than a description; it has an evocative use as we develop the language toward disclosure. In this way, Ramsey insists, talk about the "object" of a disclosure within the context of religious language becomes currency for what is objectively disclosed. Yet Ramsey does admit that in the end "in every disclosure the object can eventually bear the name 'God.' "[15]

5. Frederick Ferré, an American philosophical theologian,

in his book, *Language, Logic and God*,[16] offered an important introduction to contemporary linguistic philosophy as it bears on theological discourse. He devoted this work to a critical analysis of the "family background" of the major ways of doing philosophy, the logic of the major ways of doing theology and the functions of theological discourse. He then concludes with a presentation of his own theory of religious language and knowledge—"metaphysical models of personal activity." Ferré offers a comprehensive study of most of the contributors to the making of modern analytic philosophical theology including the existentialists, neoorthodox, neo-Thomists and both positivists and logical empiricists. And, of course, he gives a brief but incisive criticism of Ramsey. He notes Ramsey's use of the logical oddness of theological discourse which serves to evoke a distinctly theological situation (disclosure) and results in personal commitment. And after sketching—all too hastily— Ramsey's theory of God-talk, Ferré zeroes in on the same charge leveled by Lewis, namely the latent subjectivism of Ramsey's theories. Ferré quoted Ramsey as admitting the emotional nature of a religious situation, yet as "emphasizing" that all situations have an objective reference and are "*subject-object*" in structure that provides objective "depth" along with subjective feeling. Ferré claims that Ramsey merely "emphasized" his view and did not defend it, and charges Ramsey with confusing the "experiencing *as* objective" with having experience *of* the objective.[17]

6. Ninian Smart attacked Ramsey on two fronts, first in a paper "Paradox in Religion,"[18] and second in an article "The Intellectual Crisis of British Christianity."[19] In his first attack on Ramsey, Smart objected to the lack of means to falsify any disclosure or to invalidate any model in religion. He argued that on Ramsey's theory a Buddhist could use a disclosure to assert that the ultimate was impersonal or even that silence was the ultimate, and that a model for God could be an object. Smart urged that any explication of religious discourse as disclosure must give reasons for choosing one set of applicable doc-

trines rather than another. Indeed, he asked how Ramsey would answer the atheist in spite of his dictum that the "I" and "God" are "logical kinsmen," since our personal existence is not in dispute, but God's existence is.

Smart's second attack on Ramsey's views was made in an article which included all the "analyses (or supposed analyses) of religious language which made its meaning look strange . . . [and] have proved quite incapable of providing a secret defence of Christianity."[20] Smart notes the "engineering function" of Ramsey's theories; that is, by the use of qualified models and a process of negation, disclosure and commitment we are engineered toward a tautology of "I am I," but "more" than an observable person, which ultimately confirms "God." However, it is not simply the analysis qua analysis which concerns Smart, it is Ramsey's insistence on the nondescriptive evoking of disclosures as the sole function of religious language. Smart counters with the claim that some religious language is descriptive. Indeed he says, "If we take the descriptions away, we take truth away. This is why Ramsey's position, though it so far need not entail atheism, is compatible with it." And he concludes that if for Ramsey " 'God' becomes a name for penny-dropping experiences . . . Ramsey thus has really dispensed with transcendence . . . [and] God becomes finite and of this world. This is equivalent to superstitious atheism."[21] And finally, Smart contends that Ramsey has not defended himself against Ferré's charge of mere subjectivism and presses a demand for verification or criteria of objectivity.

Ramsey's reply, written simply under the title of "A Letter to the Editor,"[22] is a short but pungent apologia. He begins by reminding Smart of his reasons for writing *Religious Language*, i.e., to show that religious language is more than descriptive discourse and that "what there is" is not restricted to empirical facts, in order to meet attacks on Christianity and its apologetics. Ramsey also reminds Smart of the availability of his other writings, namely *Models and Mystery*, *On Being Sure in Religion* and *Science and Religion* in which he has expanded his views on objectivity and verification. Further, Ramsey suggests that his theory of disclosure arising from qualified models does provide an adequate way of being articulate about God, and points to his verification concept of "empirical fit" as a guarantee of his claim for objectivity. Ramsey admitted that it is a complicated issue and that he has not worked the matter out satisfactorily, but he insisted his efforts should reveal why he considered "it to be more exciting than true to call [him] an atheist."[23] Indeed in a later article,[24] Ramsey, still referring to Smart's attack, confirms that his use of "cosmic disclosures" is not just talking about ourselves or our own experiences, but a revelation of something (one) of whose existence we are aware because we have been confronted with something (one) "declaring" itself to us. In *Christian Discourse*[25] Ramsey identifies God as the objectivity that declares itself to us, in a manner similar to the declaration of duty or the moral law. Thus he admits that we "reach" some facts by the process of selection, but other facts disclose themselves to us. While Ramsey does not address Smart's charge about the lack of transcendence in his theory, in a later response to an article by Paul van Buren, Ramsey notes that it is the element of objectivity and transcendence that differentiates his position from that of van Buren, and without which the topic of Christian education would be a mere facade.[26]

7. R. B. Braithwaite, Ted Bastian and Joan Miller all wrote reviews of Ramsey's *Models and Mystery* which were printed along with a Reply by Ramsey in *Theoria to Theory*.[27] Braithwaite begins by criticizing most of Ramsey's key concepts as imprecise, especially disclosure (discernment/insight) and model. He points out that Ramsey's use of these terms has no exact usage in scientific language and calls "models" either theories or hypotheses. Further, Braithwaite notes that the insight of a scientist which prompts a conjectured hypothesis is not "disclosed" as true or false, but awaits the test of "deductive experimental verification." Braithwaite comes down hard on Ramsey's verification method of "empirical fit" or "harmoni-

zing events to hand," insisting that neither satisfies the confirmation criterion. Where then, asks Braithwaite, is the objectivity of disclosure which would motivate "commitment" (another key concept of Ramsey)? Certainly for Ramsey to insist that " 'God' is a key word, an irreducible posit, an ultimate of explanation expressive of the kind of commitment [the religious man] professes . . . "[28] will hardly answer Braithwaite. Actually he concludes, "the sincere attempt to follow Ramsey's instruction may, as it does for many religiously minded people, lead to a disclosure not of something in any way 'beyond,' but of something for which 'within' is by far the most appropriate metaphor."[29]

Joan Miller also focuses on the ambiguity of Ramsey's meaning and use of "model" and more specifically disclosure models. His attempted explications she criticizes as "obscure." Indeed, she writes, "My major criticism of this book is that Ramsey nowhere provides us with criteria for judging when a disclosure has . . . been made, in any objective way,"[30] and yet she points out that Ramsey insists that "for me the very aptness of the word I use—disclosure—is that the objective reference is safeguarded, for the object declares its objectivity by actively confronting us."[31] Miller also notes that she cannot discover in the book what Ramsey means by "empirical fit" hence she conjectures that it might mean how a given situation fits Ramsey's feelings and views of the world. Ted Bastian describes *Models and Mystery* as an apologia for what Bastian calls "sermon talk" or "any personalistic/theistic language whose use . . . has not been explained or justified." Bastian also is critical of Ramsey's use of his key terms, i.e., *disclosure* and *model*. He points out that scientists expect to use models which specify the facts precisely, that there is a virtual one-to-one correspondence of model and the facts as they really are. Bastian points out that while Ramsey does refer to cases of descriptive or picture models, what he really must do is to thoroughly explain his use of disclosure models since "we find no adequate background for the idea of disclosure from the sciences."[32]

Ramsey replied courteously and humbly to his three critics, calling his efforts an attempt to give a logic to theological "stammering." He tried to answer Miller's question, "What is a disclosure?" with a repetition of his oft-used example of the story of David and Nathan emphasizing the objective as well as the subjective features of the situation. Ramsey also tried to justify his use of models on the grounds that the word carries overtones which enable us to understand something that at the moment puzzles us. Against Bastian, Ramsey holds that explanations do have an analogy with human experience and insists that Bastian missed Ramsey's point about "pictorial" and "disclosure" models. Ramsey shows that the reference in disclosure is a given, be it the universe or God. And while he concluded with a statement of gratitude for the helpful criticisms of "my friends," it is doubtful that his defense was convincing to them.

8. John Macquarrie in his book, *God-Talk: An Examination of the Language and Logic of Theology*,[33] lauded Ramsey for his consistent characterization of religious language within religious situations stressing both discernment and commitment. Macquarrie pointed out that Ramsey, like "ourselves," sets religious language in its proper ontological context thus preserving "a faithful understanding of its own mysterious topic."[34] Macquarrie then compared his own interest in "empirical" analyses of theological language (an interest he described as existentialist), "that is to say, our first-hand participation in the experiences and situations which theology seeks to explicate," to Ramsey's "broader" empiricism, "the kind of disclosures of which Ramsey talks."[35] Macquarrie concluded that "this is something very like what I have called the 'intuiting' of situations through existential participation."[36]

9. Langdon Gilkey in his book, *Naming the Whirlwind: The Renewal of God-Language*,[37] also paid tribute to Ramsey. He wrote, "The most lively form of contemporary philosophical theology . . . [is] based on the methods and practices of ordinary language philosophy. . . . [And] is centered mainly in

Great Britain . . . [with] a number of distinguished names, headed surely by Archbishop [sic], (of Durham) Ian Ramsey. . . ." Gilkey also noted that while Ramsey held that religious language was intimately related both to moral attitudes and to self-involvement, he was well aware of the difference between each of these human phenomena, as compared to Braithwaite and van Buren. Gilkey pointed out that Ramsey's special understanding is illustrated "by the way . . . moral and existential commitment is related to the fundamental assertions about reality which religious language inevitably makes."[38] Further, Gilkey remarked that Ramsey (along with his pupil Donald Evans) exhibited the best understanding of the special nature of mystery and ultimacy in human experience which gives religious language its "odd" character appropriate to its unique dimension in experience.

C. The Later Criticisms

1. F. Michael McLain's article, "From Odd-Talk to God-Talk,"[39] called Ramsey's effort to wed theological reflection and linguistic analysis based on a possible parallel between the logic of the words "I" and "God" "creative and influential." However, while McLain approves of Ramsey's move to overcome the logical empiricist's account of self drawn mostly from Hume and also from Ryle, he criticizes Ramsey for overemphasizing the mystical nature of the self and thus identifying a dualism he certainly did not intend to posit—an objective-observable and a subjective-unobservable. While McLain admits that "I" is "more" than the observable behavior of a person, yet he argues that the something more may be described in the language of intentionality. He notes that "I do not 'discover' my intentions. I form them in the light of my situation and the reasons I have for taking one course of action as opposed to another."[40] Later, he adds the concept of activity to intention as categories which designate "I" or self by describing ("linguifying") it, without necessarily objectifying it.

McLain also criticizes Ramsey for his analogical move from
I-talk to God-talk. Here, McLain protests that it is hardly possible for something so utterly mysterious (the I) to serve as an
analogy for anything (God). Further he argues that while the
need for an adequate account of the self is an important matter
for theology, Ramsey's "lumping" the self and God together
as mystical is misleading and in the end useless. And as the
extreme "private-I" conception could lead to solopsism, so the
"knowledge" of God will be indistinguishable from self and
any certainty we would claim would be "surely not of a relationship to a reality *other than* myself."[41] McLain concludes that
it is important to understand the limitations on the usefulness
for theology of merely linguistic considerations, or of attention
to the "logic" of religious language to maintain and explain
the necessary transcendence in theological discourse.

2. Donald Evans, in his two-part article, "Ian Ramsey on
Talk About God,"[42] offers a comprehensive and constructive
critique of Ramsey's work and gives an overall review of Ramsey's major themes gathered from practically all of his books
and articles. In this way Evans, by constructing and synthesizing
Ramsey's work as a whole, fulfilled his stated reason for writing
the *Religious Studies* article, that he felt Ramsey had not done
justice to himself. Evans's main criticism of Ramsey centers
on what he judges to be Ramsey's failure to provide the criteria
for precisely deciding "empirical fit," which Evans calls "the
issue of rational preference." For instance, Evans notes that
Ramsey does not allow any model or disclosure to have priority
over his trustworthiness model or his cosmic disclosure of trustworthiness, regardless of the competing "empirical fit" of another disclosure. Pursuing this point, Evans notes that when
Ramsey applies "infinitely" to loving, he tells us in "Paradox
in Religion" to "think away any imperfect, finite, limited features." Yet Evans asks, "How does he [Ramsey] know what
counts as an imperfection in love?" Further, Evans, observing
that Ramsey selects "insights" which are the "ultimate" or
"most significant" with respect to the universe, asks how he

can do this. Evans locates Ramsey's criteria for rational preference in Christian tradition, metaphysical criteria and human
experience, but he adds immediately that Ramsey's account
of religious language would be improved with reference to "a
more profound philosophical anthropology . . ." focusing specifically on the question, "What are our most significant insights
concerning *man*?"[43] Nevertheless Evans concluded his article
by acknowledging that Ramsey's account of talk about God
is a major contribution to contemporary philosophy of religion.

3. H. P. Owen wrote a very favorable article on Ramsey,
"The Philosophical Theology of I. T. Ramsey,"[44] hailing him
for his original theory of religious language and his distinguished service to Christian philosophy. Owen observed (as
had Evans) a similarity between Ramsey's theory of qualified
models and the Thomist doctrine of analogical predication but
noted that Ramsey offered a unique restatement of the doctrine
of analogy. Owen also lauded Ramsey's apologetical efforts
to be faithful to both Scripture and Christian tradition with
very little of the extreme liberalism that mars Protestant and
Anglican theology, e.g., a reductionism to concepts acceptable
to "modern" man, or concepts "relevant" to the contemporary
condition of man. Owen also noted, with Macquarrie, that Ramsey's teaching, albeit deeply Christian, combined the best in
both empiricism and existentialism. Owen wrote,

> His theology is empirical in so far as he shows how our symbols of
> God have roots in finite experience and are qualified in ways for which
> we can produce finite analysis. Equally his theology is existentialist in
> so far as he insists that the disclosure of God occurs through personal
> situations, and that it demands an appropriate commitment. At the same
> time he avoids any tendency to equate theistic statements with their
> empirical grounds or to assume that the latter constitute verification of
> the former. Also he avoids the irrationalism and obscurity by which
> much existentialist theology is marred.[45]

4. Keith E. Yandell, in his book, *Basic Issues in the Philosophy of Religion*,[46] noting several theories of religious language,

including those of David Cox, R. B. Braithwaite, and John
Wisdom, concludes that Ramsey "in several small books, provides a distinctive theory of religious language which endeavors
to compromise between the traditional approach in which theological statements made straightforward claims and the verifica-
tionist approach in which they make no [sensible] claims at
all."[46] After developing Ramsey's theory of qualified models,
discernment and commitment sympathetically, Yandell then
turns to Ramsey's theory of disclosure and his discussion of
the "I" (self-awareness) and the awareness of God. Basically
Yandell agrees with Ramsey that the insight we have into self
is "the meeting place *par excellence* of models and mystery"
and that by speaking of self in ordinary language we can by
means of a disclosure model describing contexts (stories) develop the concept until the insight comes that self is "empirical
and more." Yet Yandell argues that Ramsey offers no proof
that his analysis of self awareness is correct or that any insight
of self awareness beyond the observable is more than a delusion,
or that the language of indescribability is not nonsense. Further,
Yandell also challenges Ramsey's move from "I" to "God."
He points out that even if the logical move is justifiable, still
the empirical claim of objectivity simply cannot be justified
since the subject "God" is even more indescribable than the
subject "I." Indeed, Yandell argues that Ramsey's "difficulty
of saying clearly what is meant by denying that the subject-
object distinction applies to disclosures plagues [his] analysis."[47] Thus Yandell concludes that appropriate religious
language is possible only if some description of God can be
meaningful and true.

   5. Cynthia B. Cohen, in two articles, "Some Aspects of Ian
Ramsey's Empiricism"[48] and "The Logic of Religious Language,"[49] offers an empathetic yet thoroughgoing critique of
Ramsey's thought. In her first article, Cohen develops Ramsey's
empirical concern for a theory of fact, emphasizing both his
concepts of "perceptual fact" (that which is sensed by the
percipient) and "disclosed fact" (that which is given to us in

a disclosure situation). Cohen argues that while some of Ramsey's disclosure situations are "anchored" in perceptual situations, many of them involve some sort of conceptual commitment, intuition or prior judgment on "fact." Indeed, Cohen contends that if Ramsey's notion that subject and object are correlative terms is accepted, Smart's charge of subjectivity of "experience" can hardly be refuted. Cohen concludes that Ramsey has ultimately "made God a mystery and mystery a God."[50]

In her second article, Cohen works out a fuller critique of Ramsey's theory of religious language. Developing some of the notions of her earlier paper, Cohen attacks Ramsey's evocative use of language rather than a more completely descriptive usage. She says,

> We cannot define solely by intuitions of situations which "go beyond" the perceived, but must become involved in analysis and judgement to evolve a satisfactory definition. To have some definition of, say, "perfection," is not to know what a particular example of a perfect thing is, but to know what it is for something to be perfect. This form of definition is dependent on reflection and judgement about a term whose meaning may be intuitively clear enough initially so that we are able to recognize particular examples. Analysis of this initial intuitive meaning enables us to form some concept of it and to apply the term consistently according to some principles.[51]

It is hardly enough to offer an identifiable object open only to "intuitive grasp," an ostensive definition based on a private, uncheckable activity. Cohen also criticizes Ramsey's use of qualified models as too dependent on the vagaries of the individual user and thus not a "logical" technique. Further, Cohen holds that in practice Ramsey "really" opts for a descriptive meaning and use of religious language and that he should just admit to that as a more adequate theory of religious language. Thus Cohen concludes that

> The diverse epistemological strands of religious discourse which are brought together in the language of various religious traditions must

be more clearly distinguished and explained. If the basis of all religious conceptions and language expressing these is an ontological insight into an object which "goes beyond" the perceived, such insight must be more carefully reinforced by an adequate theory of models.[52]

6. Roger Trigg, in his book, *Reason and Commitment*,[53] presents a criticism of Ramsey's emphasis on commitment and "logical oddness" in religious language, noting that both tend to separate religious language from ordinary language. He uses as an example Ramsey's discussion of the Resurrection of Christ in which he contrasts the question, "Did the Resurrection occur?" with the question, "Did the empty tomb occur?" Ramsey held that the first statement does not have the same logic as the second and indeed is in a different logical category from any other historical event. Therefore, Trigg points out that Ramsey places more emphasis on the commitment (the personal reaction) of the individual and too little on the empirical or objective features of the situation. He illustrates this with Ramsey's claim that "The truth of the Resurrection is logically integrated with our full commitment in Christ"[54] as evidence that the "very meaning of the term 'Resurrection' is also integrated with our commitment." Trigg insists, however, that the fact of the Resurrection and the witness to it is basic to early Christianity. Indeed, Trigg argues that Christians "follow Christ because they believe in the Resurrection (amongst other things). Any connection between beliefs and commitment is of the same kind in religion as in any other sphere of life."[55] Thus Trigg concludes that Ramsey's emphasis on religious language as "logically odd" and different from "straightforward" language is mistaken because it separates it from ordinary language and limits it to one uniform type—the commitment of an individual to a disclosure situation. Trigg insists that religious language is ordinary language used mostly in a descriptive way, especially dealing with events, and also that it will include poetry, technical theology and historical statements.

7. J. W. McClendon, Jr., and J. M. Smith, both in their

paper, "Ian Ramsey's Model of Religious Language: A Qualified Appreciation,"[56] and their book, *Understanding Religious Convictions*,[57] offer a critical review of the work of Ramsey which is at the same time "a qualified appreciation" and an extensive criticism. McClendon and Smith first question Ramsey's theory of disclosure. They ask, "Can 'disclosure' . . . account for the many strands of religion which appear in biblical history? For Saul among the prophets? and for the religion of the author of Ecclesiastes? . . . and for ecstasies of the first century Corinthians?"[58] McClendon and Smith also question the relationship of commitment to disclosure in Ramsey's theory of religious language. Noting that Ramsey would say that discernment and commitment arise together, they ask precisely how this occurs. Indeed, they argue that Ramsey has not provided a logical necessity for this relationship, simply a psychological necessity for it. Further McClendon and Smith ask, "Why is it that *all* the language of religion must consist of analog or disclosure models? . . . Why may not religious language consist of picture models as well?" Certainly, they argue, "it seems that every religious speaker speaks in straightforward ways and is at these times liable in his religious talk to be straightforwardly mistaken."[59] McClendon and Smith also point out that Ramsey himself allowed for some basic "posits" or "keywords" (such as "God") beyond his qualified model theory and conclude that religious talk cannot consist of models and qualifiers alone. Finally, McClendon and Smith charge that Ramsey's justification criterion of "empirical fit" does not meet the broader, more abstract demand for justifying religious language in general.

8. Peter Donovan's criticism of Ramsey's thought and contribution is presented in his book *Religious Language*.[60] And while Donovan's commentary on and critique of Ramsey's works is brief, the criticisms are quite telling and pointed. He first examines the nature of Ramsey's concept of disclosure. Noting that Ramsey claims to provide "empirical anchorage" in disclosure situations, Donovan asks whether the experiences

described by metaphors like "the light dawning" or "the penny dropping" are in any way more than of psychological interest, and whether such experiences give genuine information about or real discernment of anything. Donovan insists that "Ramsey's theory makes meaningfulness turn entirely on the evocative power of certain combinations of words. He fails to show how they can also be informative."[61] Donovan's second question is, granted that Ramsey's cosmic disclosures are similar to certain kinds of mystical consciousness of "higher" levels of reality produced by paradox or meditation, What is the actual content of such a mystical experience or discernment? He adds that Ramsey's evoking disclosures fails to provide both the necessary information and the objectivity to answer the question. Finally, Donovan also criticizes Ramsey for failing in the end to provide an empirically anchored foundation for religious statements since no account is (or can be) given of how facts beyond the perceived world can be known or spoken about. He concludes that "it is necessary to challenge the empiricist challenge head-on, and see if religious claims, taken in some sense descriptive and cognitive, can be shown testable and open to confirming and disconfirming observations within human life and experience."[62]

9. Terrence W. Tilley, both in an article, "Ian Ramsey and Empirical Fit"[63] and in a book, *Talking of God*,[64] presents a favorable yet knowledgeable critique of Ramsey's theory of religious language. The thesis of his article is this: the claim that Ramsey had no criteria for the justification of religious language is wrong. While there are weaknesses, Ramsey does give a complete theory and justification of God-talk.

Tilley notes Ramsey's criteria for justification: a rational/ metaphysical criterion in which consistency, simplicity, comprehensiveness and coherence make possible a reliable metaphysical "map"; a material criterion, in which Ramsey's theory of "empirical fit" makes possible the right choice of models; and a pragmatic criterion, in which a response to a cosmic disclosure expressed in a qualified model yields not only discernment, but also commitment. Tilley points out that Ramsey ranked theism highly as measured against the rational/metaphysical criterion because of its relative simplicity and immense coherence and comprehensiveness, but he observes that Ramsey correctly omitted mentioning theism's consistency. Tilley's comment on the empirical criterion is that it was not quite so straightforward, and further, while he agreed that the concept of "empirical fit" was dutifully open-ended, Tilley called the notion "vague." On the question of the pragmatic criterion, Tilley suggests that Ramsey seemed genuinely interested in the pragmatic test. In early mimeographed lecture notes he had called "By their fruits you shall know them" a sound test of truth. Yet, is the pragmatist's test the best criterion for the way we must live as Christians or to justify talk of God?

Tilley also comes to Ramsey's defense on the matter of Smart's early charge that Ramsey was virtually an atheist who simply gave the name "god" to "bits of experience" or "penny-dropping experiences." He comments that Ramsey countered with an article, "A Personal God,"[65] which gives justifications for believing in the theist's God—for instance, cosmic situations of a disclosure kind whose patterns are roughly the same as disclosures of personal reciprocity. Tilley shows that Ramsey placed much of the burden of justifying belief in a personal God on the validity of religious experience of the "reciprocally active" encounter of persons and in the cosmic disclosure of the "other" person evoked. And while Tilley admits that the argument falters in that it assumes what is at issue: that there is something to respond to in responding to God, nevertheless it does show how important persons are to Ramsey. Indeed, Tilley describes Ramsey's conviction that "as persons are not bundles of events but centers of activity, so the world is not a bundle of events but the arena of activity where God and persons meet and interact"—in a personal response.[66]

D. A Gentle Assessment

1. A Summary of the Major Criticisms and Personal Evaluations

(a) Braithwaite offered an early challenge to Ramsey's empirical grounding of religious language. He complains about the
way Ramsey uses "empirical" and "fact" and notes that Ramsey
uses inverted commas around *fact* to emphasize that such language is logically odd and needs logical qualifiers. Braithwaite
then asks, What is odd logic? and How does one teach it to
a non-Christian? Edwards comments that this could be one
of Ramsey's major weaknesses. And Donovan questions
whether Ramsey's philosophical theology is really empirical
in the usual sense of the word.

As a philosopher I have to agree with Ramsey's critics. I
do understand Ramsey's notion of a "wider" empiricism and
acknowledge that both Locke and Berkeley yearned for such
an epistemological category. Nevertheless it was an anomaly
in Locke and a paradox in Berkeley and not fully explained
nor justified in Ramsey.

(b) Lewis charged that Ramsey's reference to God as the
objective counterpart to "I" is inconclusive. Smart also chal-
lenged Ramsey's concept of "I" and "God" as logical analogs.
Smart points out that our existence is not in dispute, but God's
existence is. Further, Smart argues that Ramsey may insist
on a logical relationship of the two terms, yet Ramsey assumes
empirical reality. And Smart concludes, Where is the transcendence in Ramsey's argument from self? McLain also is concerned with Ramsey's analogical move from self to God. He
insists that Analogy cannot sustain a claim for any reality beyond the self—and yet this is what is needed in religious language. Yandell adds that Ramsey offers no proof of his analysis
of self-awareness and notes that intuition or insight beyond
observability may be either illusion or nonsense.

On the matter of Ramsey's clever and insightful way of
encouraging an understanding of both the extended self and

the special "Self" which men call "God," I find it a helpful
way of talking about God. And while I must agree with Ramsey's
critics in the end that the logical, analogical move does not
establish an existent divine reality, God; nevertheless this analogy does help to clarify how religious belief is related to a
dimension of human experience which cannot be identified with
any specific or finite list of observable data. It is in this demand
of the subjectivity of self for some kind of transcendence, projected to its logical analog "God," which I find helpful in
explaining God-talk.

(c) Ferré charged Ramsey with latent subjectivism, of confusing experiencing *as* objective with having an experience *of*
the objective. Smart in his later critique observes that Ferré's
charge has not been answered by Ramsey. Braithwaite asks
Ramsey, "Where is the objectivity of disclosure?" And Trigg
calls attention to Ramsey's emphasis on personal (subjective)
response and his failure to develop the objective features of
the situation.

Ramsey's replies called attention to his later writings, developing a fuller view of objectivity and a growing emphasis on
God-talk as a disclosure of something "declaring" itself. And
in a later response to van Buren Ramsey insists on both objectivity and transcendence in religion. Actually Ramsey endeavored
in his later works to rehabilitate the concept of the transcendent
from within (or perhaps in spite of) the standpoint of empiricism. Most of his major concepts, i.e., the "more," disclosure,
commitment, qualified models, and so on, are in fact his elaboration of what he perceives to be the lived-experience of transcendence.

Certainly Ramsey was aware of the inadequacy of the explanations his theory offered to believing Christians and non-be-
lievers alike, but his discernment-commitment mechanism was
based on a subjective response to an empirically unidentifiable
objective referent. I am confident that Ramsey, in the company
of many Christian (or idealist) philosophers, held that some
cognitive states are perceived as objective, and that Ramsey

would say with Browning (in "Abt Vogler"), " 'Tis we musicians [Christians] know." Such a conclusion is not foreign to Wittgenstein's injunction to assess the meaning from the use.

(d) Smart provided the cruelest criticism of all: that Ramsey's insistence on nondescriptive religious language is compatible with atheism since only descriptive language preserves the straightforward truth of theism. Cohen attacks Ramsey's evocative use of language and charges that it is inadequate to offer an object open only to an intuitive grasp and models dependent on the vagaries of the user.

On the subject of the meaning and validity of religious language, I find that most discussions put forward by the strict logical empiricists ignore the fact that language develops and is used within the context of one's culture. Thus there are no absolute meanings—a truth that is just as obvious in science as it is in religion. In many places Ramsey made this linguistic phenomenon quite clear. Therefore, in religion, as in every other interest of man, the use of language prescribes several kinds of statements, including descriptive (Jesus was born in Bethlehem), evaluative (Christians ought to love one another), and evocative (a disclosure model calls for our commitment). I perceive Ramsey's use of religious language as inclusive not exclusive.

Both Owen and Tilley defend Ramsey against the criticism of atheism. Owen says Ramsey is keenly aware of divine transcendence and Tilley uses Ramsey's article, "A Personal God," to show his orthodoxy. I am convinced that Ramsey was indeed an orthodox Christian. Yet like Owen I would include him in the "liberal" wing of Anglican Protestantism, using that word in the good sense of the word *liberal*. Ramsey practiced and defended intellectual inquiry, the use of both faith and reason as well as the philosophical tools of the secular academic community. But he was definitely not "a superstitious atheist."

(e) Smart also criticized Ramsey's lack of providing means to falsify any disclosure or invalidate any model. Braithwaite took Ramsey to task for using his key words (*disclosure, model,* and so on) imprecisely (Miller says ambiguously). Bastian calls attention to the fact that he finds no adequate background from the sciences to support Ramsey's disclosure. Cohen distinguishes "perceptual" from "disclosure" fact and then points out that many cosmic disclosures depend on prior conceptual commitment or intuition. McClendon and Smith question Ramsey's use of disclosure as accounting for all religious representation. Further, they also question the relation of discernment and commitment to disclosure and ask if they really do arise together. Finally, Donovan asks, Is disclosure any more than of psychological interest? For instance, is it in any way informative? And what is the content of discernment?

No one answer will satisfy all these diverse but related questions about Ramsey's key terms. Obviously, there are those who consider Ramsey's theories and terminology inadequately explained. However, many others, including Jerry Gill, Owen, Tilley and myself, consider that Ramsey has carefully and adequately developed and explained a system or theory of religious language. I am concerned more specifically with the several challenges to Ramsey's assumption that ordinary experience (and even scientific experience) is common to all language and knowledge, and that, therefore, religious language and knowledge may be established as meaningful by a contextually experiential process. Indeed, the light may dawn and the penny drop in the scientific method signifying the presence of disclosure, and perhaps discernment and commitment, in that pristine process. Further, I might point out that Ramsey's theory of religious language has been a significant factor in the development of philosophical theology for more than two decades at this writing.

(f) Braithwaite also criticized Ramsey's concept of "empirical fit" or "harmonizing events to hand" as an inadequate mode of verification. Miller notes the lack of adequate criteria for the concept and comments that Ramsey's feelings and views of the world would hardly do. Bastian calls Ramsey's thought "sermon-talk," by which he means any unexplained or unjusti-

fied talk. McClendon and Smith argue that "empirical fit" just
does not meet the broader demand for verification. And Tilley
admits that the concept is not straightforward and calls it
"vague."

Ramsey would readily admit that verification in religious
knowledge is difficult and that he borrowed from Max Black
the determination of the goodness of a model's "fit" (with
the facts of human experience). Ramsey would apply the concept
to every question of religious knowledge (coming from human
experience). And while some point out the possible subjectivism
of the procedure, Ramsey counterattacks with a new word to
suit the mechanism, "intersubjective," by which he means subjective with an objective element or "outward" feature. The
concept may be helpful in some situations, but it is hardly
verification in the strict sense of that word.

I find it both healthy and helpful that Ramsey admitted
readily that theism is not a scientific hypothesis whose empirical
success and reliability is measured by the extent to which the
deductions made from it are experimentally verified. And I
also find it useful to turn to his description of the task of
the theologian as ascertaining how his theory "fits" a particular
situation, its qualified models and disclosures, which will provide a better-fitting conceptual framework for the knowledge
and understanding of God. Further, Ramsey's likening the theologian to the archaeologist, anthropologist, or even the detective, I find interesting and illuminating on the process of the
rational preference for choosing the better "fit" of available
theories.

(g) McLain criticizes Ramsey's overemphasis on the mystical
element of "self" and the seeming dualism which develops
between the objective-observable and the subjective-unobservable. And McLain suggests the language of intentionality and
personal activity to explain the "more" beyond observability.

Ramsey is open to some criticism at this point simply because
he does not clearly identify the superempirical element in the
self. Certainly I understand Ramsey's reluctance (or inability)

to define it, yet reference to other philosophers and psychologists and their theories of mind and self might have been helpful, especially since the nonobservable element in self Ramsey names as the logical pointer to God. However, I would like to point out that McLain and Ramsey are more in agreement than McLain recognizes. First, Ramsey's early concern with a criticism of Hume and Ryle was replaced later with the development of his own position of self-knowledge as a *via media* between behaviorism and Cartesianism, but never "utterly mysterious." Second, Ramsey's later works, most notably *Models for Divine Activity*, do seem to reflect his interest in the notions of intentionality and activity, held by McLain to be helpful in explicating self-awareness.

(h) Trigg argues that Ramsey's overemphasis on subjective commitment and "logical oddness" in religious language will eventually lead to its separation from ordinary language and thus to its ultimate meaninglessness. Trigg would have support from many other linguistic analysts on this criticism. I am inclined to agree with them in principle, if in fact Trigg accurately describes Ramsey's theory of religious language. However, I perceive that Ramsey follows Wittgenstein in his theory of use as meaning. Ramsey is well aware that meaning arises from the employment of language for various purposes, i.e., naming, describing, prescribing, and so on. Therefore, I believe that Ramsey is describing a fact of linguistic reality, i.e., that while religious language is ordinary language, many religious terms and statements are not straightforward descriptive language. Thus I find Ramsey's map for understanding the terrain of religious language useful and propose that someday it may be judged indispensable.

(i) McClendon and Smith question whether all religious discourse consists of analog or disclosure models. Indeed, they ask why may not religious language consist of picture models as well? And they hasten to add that Ramsey gives no linguistic reason to deny this possibility and note that Ramsey himself talks of certain key words (*God, Spirit,* and so on) which are not analog models. Thus McClendon and Smith answer their own question. Happily Ramsey does identify some nonanalog models, yet for him the burden of religious utterance is borne by qualified models.

(j) Evans points out a weakness in Ramsey's thought which I think is quite significant: Ramsey's failure to deal with the latest philosophical, psychological, sociological and anthropological insights concerning man. Evans says Ramsey needs a more profound philosophical anthropology to illumine what he believes about human nature, community, trust, hope, commitment and love. I believe Ramsey would be in agreement with Evans's prescription, yet Ramsey was moving in this direction when he suggested that the language of faith is confirmed through the way this language gives rise to and sustains a community.

2. A Few Concluding Commendations

(a) Ramsey As a Philosopher

I came away from Oxford in 1964 with the highest regard for Ian Ramsey. He had fulfilled my highest expectations. I had been with him, worked with him and shared conferences and seminars with him. Further, I had been inspired by him to develop two germ-ideas into successful papers, "Moral-Spiritual Values"[67] and "On the Relations Between Morals and Religion."[68] In all of his tutoring and working conferences I found him to have almost an encyclopedic grasp of both subject matter and the related bibliographic materials. Yet he was markedly humble and eager to pass on every credit to his pupil. His influence at Oxford was immediately obvious. His notes won me interviews with Ryle, Hare, Ayer and others, and access to libraries and other resources so useful to a fellowship scholar. From Hare I learned that Ramsey had won a great amount of good will and the sincere respect of his colleagues.

One resource which Ramsey shared with me as a lecturer in Philosophy of Religion was his mimeographed notes which he entitled simply, "Introduction to the Philosophy of Religion." They were immediately helpful to me, since they demonstrated the practical use Ramsey's theory and key terms have for the main concerns of religion and religious language—for instance, Ramsey's section in which he considers "The Traditional Arguments for the Existence of God." Immediately he admits these deductive arguments are worthless in proving God's existence. However, Ramsey would not dispense with them for they provide either techniques by which to evoke a cosmic disclosure (Anselm's "that than which nothing greater can be conceived"), or hints as to the logical behavior of the word *God*, i.e., how to speak of God in relation to what is disclosed objectively in a disclosure situation. (Necessary being suggests that *God* must be regarded as a key word whose existence is guaranteed by informed irreversible inference from a qualified model.)

Ramsey similarly deals with miracles, evil and immortality. He suggests that a miracle is a particular configuration of events giving rise to a disclosure on the basis of which we use the language of the special personal activity of God. For Ramsey, miracles are places *par excellence* where personal language about God is grounded and he uses the phrase "Personal decisive activity" of God, as illustrated by the New Testament claim that God "raised" Jesus from the dead. It is extremely encouraging that Ramsey insisted that both scientific and theological accounts of miracles are not only necessary but also not incompatible to preserve our sense of God's transcendence. The scientific understanding of a miracle situation supplements and balances the divine activity account to promote elucidation.

On the subject of evil, Ramsey says that the most attractive solutions to the problem of evil convert to the problem of ascribing *purposes* or (even better) *attributes* to God. To solve the latter problem we need to use qualifiers to evoke a disclosure and so create the necessary affirmation of God. For Ramsey the only way to "explain" evil is to face it, *viz.*, to embody it into one's overall religious loyalty, as compared to an attempt

to deal piecemeal with particular evil. His theodicy is based
on a personal model, the Christ of the cross who illuminates
redeeming love and discloses the sacramental character of suffering (and death). And while this special model can in fact
evoke a disclosure of God's love and purpose, Ramsey insisted
that the "mystery" of God and evil is something no model
fits perfectly. Still, he concludes that evil and suffering are
crucial occasions *par excellence* for knowing both God and ourselves.

Ramsey points out that immortality is best understood by
regarding the term as a qualified model in which the prefix
"im" acts as a qualifier, i.e., to spur us to press on with our
stories until a disclosure is evoked which reveals that we are
more than our mortality. For Ramsey, therefore, immortality
is justified by the logical analogy between the observable objective "I" and the "I" which is something "more" which cannot
be restricted to objects. The statement, "the soul is immortal,"
Ramsey points out, contains both prescription and description.
However, Ramsey's unique analysis is that the statement combines them in such a way that, being evocative, it is grounded
in a situation which transcends the verifiable criteria it contains.
Ramsey also holds that the Christian assertion, "I have eternal
life in Christ Jesus our Lord," combines both subjective and
objective elements. And he notes that its claim and appeal
are based on the distinctive disclosure situation in which it
is grounded.

Certainly these Ramseyan statements may not solve all of
the philosophical problems inherent in the main concerns of
religion, still they do go a long way to illuminating a helpful
method of examining and dealing with the problem areas and
their language dilemmas. The value of Ramsey's philosophy
of religion for me is that it is loyal to the analytic method of
doing philosophy described elsewhere as a laborious effort to
criticize and clarify the foundations of our beliefs, while remaining loyal to the interests of the problems of religion. His notes,
for example, examine carefully the positions of friend and foe

on all the problems I have mentioned above, and then present his own views, i.e., self-disclosure, with careful elucidation, illustration, and a consideration of the possible objections of rival views. Ramsey's attractiveness as a philosopher of religion can be seen in the final words of his Introductory Lecture: "Here is the empirical basis for religion, and the rest of the course will . . . show how the traditional topics and problems of the philosophy of religion can be treated by reference to such a situation [of disclosure] as we have indicated."[69]

The importance of Ramsey as a philosophical theologian stems from the fact that he is both a capable philosopher—a fact established by his excellent introduction to Locke's *The Reasonableness of Christianity*, which he edited and abridged—and an ingenious theologian, a claim established by his clever efforts to relate his philosophically inspired theories and constructs to his view of the Christian faith in accordance with both biblical and traditional theology. Further, he was always ready and willing to enter into dialogue and discussion with both philosophers (analytic and existential) and theologians (liberal and conservative) to enlighten both disciplines and secure for theology the application of the tools of analytic philosophy toward the construction of a new philosophical theology. It was Ramsey's hope to provide the catalyst which would replace "natural theology" and "revealed theology" (alone) with a grounding in the kind of experience (his "disclosure") which would make meaningful religious language possible. Ramsey concludes his article, "Contemporary Empiricism," with an enthusiastic claim that empiricism "may even yet revitalize 'theological thinking' as it has revolutionalized philosophy."[70]

(b) Ramsey As a Preacher

I conclude with an assessment of Ramsey as a preacher because it is my belief that Ramsey has not been given the credit he deserves for his consummate skill in communicating his erudition, self-confidence, poise and good will from the pulpit as well as from the lecture stand. Edwards compares Ramsey unfavorably with two of the Church of England's better preachers, the Rev. Canon Dr. Charles Raven, the Regius Professor of Divinity at Cambridge when Ramsey was a student, and the Rt. Rev. Dr. Michael Ramsey, Archbishop of Canterbury. I cannot say how Ian Ramsey compares with Dr. Raven, since I never heard Raven preach. But I have read his sermons and must say I prefer Ramsey's written sermons. On the comparison of Bishop Ramsey with Archbishop Ramsey as preachers, I will reluctantly agree with Edwards and for the reasons he gives, i.e., the Archbishop was learned but his presentation was smoother and more appropriate in style and speech.

Nevertheless, I found Ramsey to be an excellent preacher. His sermons were meticulously prepared and he exuded both good will and sincerity in his presentation. His style was not as declarative or as dramatic as the style of the Archbishop, but it was persuasive and heartwarming. For instance, I heard his University Sermon at St. Mary the Virgin Church, Oxford, preached on St. Barnabas Day, 14 June 1964. In his introduction, Ramsey sketched the career of Barnabas as a colleague of St. Paul and a Christian missionary of generous social conscience and broad theological influence. Ramsey noted that Barnabas should be the favorite of Professor Braithwaite and Bishop Robinson—a morally upright and loving Christian. Ramsey then spoke of the University's Christian social responsibility and its religious obligation. He pointed out the two roles of the University: first, as the dispenser of knowledge, an empirical role, which Ramsey said was hardly enough since values-discernment and decision-making capabilities are also needed; second, as the resource of unifying vision and common principles—an ethical role, which Ramsey held to be necessary to apprehend, discern, and commit us to moral and social obligation.

Ramsey then turned to the role of theology (religion) in the university. He observed that society abounded in social problems, e.g., ethical decisions in business and medicine, all of which demand the cooperation of many disciplines, including theology (religion). Indeed, Ramsey insisted that it is especially religion which can supply both the vision and the motivation to supply answers and action to our most difficult questions. For his conclusion Ramsey chose a popular song of that period, "Blowin' in the Wind" by Bob Dylan, and used it with appealing ingenuity within the framework of his theory of religious language. He noted some of the difficult questions raised in the song (i.e., how long does a mountain have to stand before it erodes into the sea, how long does a man have to live before he finds freedom, and how often can a man ignore the injustices going on around him?) as indicating that there are no cut-and-dried answers to man's moral questions. The refrain and its repetition of the words of the title, "Blowin' in the Wind," Ramsey said, supports the theme. He presented this metaphor of the model of the Holy Spirit as the Christian's guide in solving moral dilemmas. Ramsey names Barnabas as a holy man who was said to be "full of the Holy Spirit" and affirmed this to be the reason for the obvious social conscience and the stedfast conviction of that first century missionary and theologian. And his exhortation, though unspoken, was to "go and do likewise!"

Homiletical critics may argue that this was not a great sermon and some more conservative Protestants may insist that it fails almost every major test for great sermons: biblical, doctrinal, conversional and evangelical. Yet Ramsey did that which all great preachers have done and continue to do: he matched his theme with the occasion, and with attention to the Bible, church history, and theology he carefully developed a situation of need and common experience to disclose a Christian responsibility of both the university and the individuals for an informed moral and social conscience.

Such a performance is worthy of the man who in defending his use of models and qualifiers had chided Antony Flew by saying his building up of religious discourse by metaphors and models does not bring with them Flew's prediction of "death by a thousand qualifications," but as Ramsey says, "Rather it is life by a thousand enrichments."[71] Such a man merits my praise and my warm, continuing appreciation and the praise and appreciation of others.

Notes

CHAPTER I

1. This biographical sketch relies on the "summary of the life and thought" of *Ian Ramsey, Bishop of Durham: A Memoir* written by David L. Edwards and published by Oxford University Press in 1973.

2. A point of view later supported in a paper "On the Possibility and Purpose of a Metaphysical Theology," published in *Prospect for Metaphysics* which Ramsey edited, London, George Allen & Unwin, Ltd., 1961.

3. Starr King Press (The Beacon Press), Boston, 1951.

4. Published by Clarendon Press in 1952 and reprinted in *The Miracles and the Resurrection*, London, SPCK, 1964.

5. Edwards, *op. cit.*, p. 54.   6. *Ibid.*, p. 89.

7. *Ibid.*, pp. 99–101.

CHAPTER II

1. Francis Bacon, *First Book of Aphorisms*, From *The Age of Reason*, Stuart Hampshire, ed. (N.Y.: New American Library, 1956), p. 25.

2. Francis Bacon, *Essays* in *The Philosophical Works of Francis Bacon*, J. M. Robertson, ed. (London: Routledge, 1905), p. 754.

3. Quoted in Leslie Stephen, *Thomas Hobbes* (London: Macmillan, 1904), p. 77ff.

4. Thomas Hobbes, *Human Nature*, in *The English Works of Thomas Hobbes*, William Molesworth, ed. (London: Bohn, Vol. IV, 1840), p. 18.

5. Thomas Hobbes, *Leviathan*, F. B. Randall, ed. (N.Y.: Washington Square Press, 1964), p. 70.

6. *Ibid.*, p. 269.   7. *Ibid.*, p. 18.

8. John Locke, *Essay Concerning Human Understanding*, (Books II and IV) Mary W. Calkins, ed. (LaSalle, Ill.: Open Court, 1962), p. 13.

9. *Ibid.*, pp. 18–19.   10. *Ibid.*, pp. 25–26.

11. *Ibid.*, p. 267.   12. *Ibid.*, pp. 284–285.

13. Locke's *Essay*, from *The Reasonableness of Christianity*, I. T. Ramsey, ed. (London: A. and C. Black, 1958), pp. 9–10.

14. *Op. cit.*, Locke, *Essay Concerning Human Understanding*, pp. 315–318.

15. *Op. cit.*, Locke, *Essay*, from *The Reasonableness* . . . , pp. 10–11 (Book IV, Chapter 18, para. 2)

16. *Ibid.*, p. 12. (Book IV, Chapter 19, Conclusion)

17. *Ibid.*, p. 11. (Book IV, Chapter 18, para. 5)

18. George Berkeley, *A Treatise Concerning the Principles of Human Knowledge* (LaSalle, Ill.: Open Court, 1957), p. 31.

19. *Ibid.*, pp. 24–25.   20. *Ibid.*, pp. 32–33.

21. *Ibid.*, p. 120.

22. Quoted in S. E. Stumpf, *Socrates to Sartre* (N.Y.: McGraw-Hill, 1975), p. 289.

23. Ian T. Ramsey, *Models for Divine Activity* (London: SCM Press, 1973), p. 1.

24. *Op. cit.*, Berkeley, *A Treatise* . . . , p. 26.

25. *Op. cit.*, Stumpf, *Socrates to Sartre*, p. 291.

26. David Hume, *A Treatise of Human Nature* (N.Y.: Doubleday, 1961), p. 4.

27. David Hume, *An Inquiry Concerning Human Understanding*, D. W. Hendel, ed. (N.Y.: Liberal Arts Press), p. 89.

28. *Ibid.*, p. 30.

29. *Op. cit.*, Hume, *A Treatise*, p. 152.

30. *Ibid.*, p. 229.   31. *Ibid.*, p. 15.

32. *Op cit.*, Hume, *An Inquiry*, p. 173.   33. *Ibid.*, p. 155.

34. David Hume, *Dialogues Concerning Natural Religion*, H. D. Aiken, ed. (N.Y.: Hafner, 1961), p. 58.

35. *Ibid.*, p. 94.   36. *Ibid.*, p. 66.   37. *Ibid.*, p. 69.

38. David Hume, *The Natural History of Religion*, in *Hume on Religion*, Richard Wollheim, ed. (London: Collins, 1966), p. 98.

39. *Op. cit.*, Hume, *A Treatise*, p. 243.

40. A. J. Ayer, *Language, Truth and Logic* (N.Y.: Dover, 1946), p. 55.

41. See James' development of this discrimination in William James, *Pragmatism and Other Essays* (N.Y.: Washington Square Press, 1968), pp. 6–21.

42. *Ibid.*, p. 1.

43. J. S. Mill, *Auguste Comte and Positivism* (Ann Arbor, Mich.: University of Michigan Press, 1965), p. 6.

44. C. S. Peirce, "How to Make Our Ideas Clear," *Popular Science Monthly* Vol. 12 (Jan. 1878) reprinted in *The Age of Analysis*, Morton White, ed. (N.Y.: New American Library, 1955), p. 146.

45. William James, *The Meaning of Truth* (Ann Arbor, Mich: University of Michigan Press, 1970), pp. xxxvi–xxxvii.

46. *Op. cit.*, James, *Pragmatism*, p. 25.   47. *Ibid.*, p. 26.

48. *Ibid.*, p. 28.   49. *Ibid.*, p. 35.   50. *Ibid.*, p. 200.

51. *Ibid.*, p. 212.   52. *Ibid.*, p. 89.

53. John Dewey, *The Quest for Certainty* (N.Y.: Putnam, 1929), p. 37.

54. John Dewey, *Logic: The Theory of Inquiry* (N.Y.: Henry Holt, 1938), p. 461.

55. John Dewey, *The Influence of Darwin on Philosophy and Other Essays* (N.Y.: Henry Holt, 1920), p. 17.

56. John Dewey, "The Need for a Recovery of Philosophy," in *John Dewey on Experience, Nature and Freedom* (N.Y.: Liberal Arts Press, 1960), p. 23.

57. *Op. cit.*, Dewey, *The Quest*, p. 228.

58. *Op. cit.*, Dewey, *Logic*, pp. 112, 112–113 and 113–114.

59. See my book, *Decisions in Philosophy of Religion* (Columbus, Ohio: Charles Merrill, 1976), Chapter II for a full discussion of the difficulty with the term "Religion."

60. John Dewey, *A Common Faith* (New Haven: Yale University Press, 1934), p. 24.

61. *Ibid.*, pp. 43–44.   62. *Ibid.*, pp. 49–53.

63. See A. J. Ayer, *The Origins of Pragmatism* (San Francisco: Freeman–Cooper, 1968), in which Ayer attests to the successful contribution of pragmatism.

64. G. E. Moore, *Some Main Problems of Philosophy* (London: Allen & Unwin, 1953), p. 2.

65. G. E. Moore, *Principia Ethica* (London: Cambridge University Press, 1903), p. vii.

66. Bertrand Russell, *The Problems of Philosophy* (London: Oxford University Press, 1968), p. 46.

67. *Ibid.*, p. 48.   68. *Ibid.*, p. 20.

69. Bertrand Russell, "Logical Atomism," *Contemporary British Philosophy*, J. H. Muirhead, ed. (N.Y.: Macmillan, 1924), pp. 379–380.

70. See for example Russell's debate on the existence of God with Professor Frederick Copleston reprinted in my book, *Decisions in Philosophy of Religion*.

71. Bertrand Russell, *Why I Am Not a Christian*, (N.Y.: Simon & Schuster, 1957), p. v.

72. Ludwig Wittgenstein, *Tractatus Logico-Philosophicus*, C. K. Ogden and F. P. Ramsey, trans. (London: Kegan Paul, 1922), p. 4.112.

73. *Ibid.*   74. *Its Scientific World Outlook.*

75. *Op. cit.*, Wittgenstein, *Tractatus*, p. 4.024.

76. "A New Philosophy of Experience," *College of Pacific Publications* (Vol. 1, 1932).

77. *Op. cit.*, Ayer, *Language*, p. 31.   78. *Ibid.*, p. 36.

79. *Ibid.*, p. 108.   80. *Ibid.*, p. 115.   81. *Ibid.*, p. 9.

82. *Ibid.*, p. 10.

83. Ludwig Wittgenstein, *Philosophical Investigations*, G. E. M. Anscombe, trans. (Oxford: Basil Blackwell, 1953), para. 43, p. 20e.

84. *Ibid.*, para. 96, p. 44e.   85. *Ibid.*, para. 77, p. 36e.

86. *Ibid.*, para. 499–500, pp. 138–139e.

87. Reprinted in *20th-Century Philosophy: The Analytic Tradition*, Morris Weitz, ed. (N.Y.: Collier-Macmillan, 1966), pp. 203–204.

88. Gilbert Ryle, *The Concept of Mind*, (N.Y.: Barnes and Noble, 1961), p. 16.

89. W. B. Williamson, *Language and Concepts in Christian Education* (Philadelphia: Westminster Press, 1970), p. 59.

90. Gilbert Ryle, *Dilemmas* (London: Cambridge University Press, 1960), p. 11.

91. Some of the more important of these works are: Flew, A. G. N., ed., *Logic and Language* (I and II), (1951, 1953); Hare, R. M., *The Language of Morals* (1952); Braithwaite, R. B., *Scientific Explanation* (1953); Strawson, P. F., *Individuals* (1959) and *Introduction to Logical Theory* (1954); Flew, A. G. N. and MacIntyre, A., eds., *New Essays in Philosophical Theology* (1955); Urmson, J. O., *Philosophical Analysis* (1956); MacIntyre, A., ed., *Metaphysical Beliefs* (1957); Mitchell, B., ed., *Faith and Logic* (1957); Hart, H. L. A., *The Concept of Law* (1961); Austin, J. L., *How to Do Things with Words* (1962).

92. I. T. Ramsey, "Contemporary Empiricism," in *Christian Empiricism*, J. H. Gill, ed. (London: Sheldon Press, 1974), pp. 8–9.

93. *Op. cit.*, Hume, *Inquiry*, p. 19.

CHAPTER III

1. John Locke, *An Essay Concerning Human Understanding* Bk IV, Chapter 21, para. 4, p. 1.

2. Basil Blackwell, Oxford, 1951.

3. *Logic and Language I*, A. G. N. Flew, ed. (Oxford: Blackwell, 1951), pp. 2–3.

4. *Ibid.*, p. 6.

5. John Wisdom, "Gods," *Logic and Language*, p. 187.

6. *Ibid.*, pp. 188–189.   7. *Ibid.*, pp. 192–193.

8. *Ibid.*, p. 197.   9. *Ibid.*, p. 202.   10. *Ibid.*, p. 206.

11. John Wisdom, *Philosophy and Psychoanalysis* (Oxford: B. Blackwell, 1953), p. 153.

12. S. C. M. Press, London, 1953.

13. *New Essays in Philosophical Theology*, A. G. N. Flew and A. MacIntyre, eds. (London: S. C. M. Press, 1953), p. 96.

14. *Ibid.*, p. 97.   15. *Ibid.*, pp 98–99.

16. R. M. Hare, "Religion and Morals" in *Faith and Logic*, Basil Mitchell, ed. (Boston: Beacon Press, 1957), p. 179.

17. *Op. cit.*, *New Essays*, pp. 99–100.   18. *Ibid.*, p. 101.

19. David Hume, *A Treatise on Human Nature*, T. H. Green, ed. (London: Grose, 1898), p. 501.

20. *Op. cit.*, Hare, "Religion and Morals," p. 190.

21. *Op. cit.*, *New Essays*, p. 103.   22. *Ibid.*, pp. 103–104.

23. *Ibid.*, p. 105.

24. *The Problem of Religious Knowledge* (Englewood Cliffs: Prentice-Hall, 1963).

25. *The New Dialogue Between Philosophy and Theology* (New York: Seabury Press, 1966).

26. *Op. cit.*, *New Essays*, p. 106.   27. *Ibid.*, p. 107.

28. *Ibid.*, p. 108.

29. R. B. Braithwaite, "An Empiricist's View of the Nature of Religious Belief," in *Christian Ethics and Contemporary Philosophy*, I. T. Ramsey, ed. (London: S. C. M. Press, 1966), p. 53.

30. Cf., pp. 55–58.   31. *Ibid.*, p. 63.   32. *Ibid.*, p. 66.

33. *Op. cit.*, *New Essays*, p. 116.

34. Cf., I. M. Crombie, "The Possibility of Theological Statements," in *Faith and Logic*, B. Mitchell, ed. (Boston: Beacon Press, 1957), p. 60.

35. *Op. cit.*, *New Essays*, pp. 122–123.

36. *Ibid.*, p. 124.   37. *Ibid.*, pp. 128–129.

38. Alasdair MacIntyre, "The Logical Status of Religious Beliefs," in *Metaphysical Beliefs*, A. MacIntyre, ed. (London: S. C. M. Press, 1957), pp. 182, 185, 211.

39. *Ibid.*, pp. 202, 199, 200.   40. *Ibid.*, p. 209.

41. *Ibid.*, p. 193.   42. Cf., *Ibid.*, pp. 206, 207.

43. *Philosophical Quarterly*, Vol. 11, No. 44 (7/1961).

44. *Op. cit.*, *Metaphysical Beliefs*, p. 205.

45. Bernard E. Meland in his introduction to *The Future of Empirical Theology* (University of Chicago Press, 1969) offers a brief survey of the history and character of the Chicago empirical theological tradition. Meland describes in a general way how the Chicago school has drawn upon phychology, sociology and philosophy of religion so as to provide a broader base for its empiricist account of the nature of religion. After mentioning the contributions of Shailer Matthews, Gerald Birney Smith, Edward Schribner Ames and Douglas Clyde MacIntosh, Meland then singles out Wieman as the one who most deserves to be regarded as the major spokesperson of the Chicago tradition.

46. Macmillan, N. Y., 1963.

47. *The Empirical Theology of Henry Nelson Wieman*, R. W. Bretall, ed. (N.Y.: Macmillan, 1963), p. 3.

48. *Ibid.*, p. 4.   49. *Ibid.*, p. 5.

50. *Op. Cit.*, *Empirical Theology*, p. 257.

51. H. N. Wieman, *The Source of Human Good* (Chicago: University of Chicago Press, 1946), p. 367.

52. *Ibid.*, pp. 190, 303.

53. John Herman Randall, Jr., "Naturalistic Humanism," in *Patterns of Faith in America Today*, F. E. Johnson, ed. (N.Y.: Collier Books, 1962), p. 161.

54. Cf., *Ibid.*, pp. 162, 164.

55. Paul Tillich contributed to the ongoing analysis of theological language and its salvation from the veto of logical positivism by his advocacy of religious utterances as symbolical. In his *Systematic Theology* (1951) and *Theology of Culture* (1959) Tillich proposes five steps toward the clarification of the meaning of symbols. (1) Symbols are different than signs in that while both point beyond themselves to something else, only symbols participate in the reality of that to which they point. (2) The function of a symbol is thus representative, but in such a way that it opens up levels of reality otherwise hidden and unavailable, much like the "meditation" on a painting or a poem. (3) The nature of religious symbols is best expressed as a key which unlocks the depth dimension of the human soul to the ultimate ground of being. (4) There are levels of religious symbols, e.g., the transcendent level which goes beyond empirical reality. Yet, while all

God-talk is symbolic, we cannot say that God is a symbol. Indeed the one literal, nonsymbolic statement is "God is Being Itself" and all other religious language, while cognitively unverifiable, is meaningful as the vehicle for the expression of "ultimate reality," "ground of being"—of God. (5) Thus religious symbols are independent of any verification process. For Tillich, their truth is their adequacy to the religious situation in which they were created and are used. Indeed, symbols alone can express man's "ultimate concern," i.e., his faith. (Cf., "The Nature of Religious Language," *Theology of Culture*, (N.Y. Oxford University Press, 1967).

56. J. H. Randall, Jr., *The Role of Knowledge in Western Religion* (Boston: Starr King Press, 1958), pp. 114–115.

57. *Ibid.*, pp. 116, 117.   58. *Ibid.*, pp. 112, 119.

59. J. H. Randall, Book Review, *Thought*, Vol. 39, No. 155 (Winter, 1964), p. 630.

60. Frederick Ferré, *Language, Logic and God* (London: Eyre and Spottis-Woode, 1962), pp. vii, ix.

61. J. A. Martin, Jr., *The New Dialogue Between Philosophy and Theology* (N.Y.: Seabury Press, 1966), p. 168.

62. Op. cit., Ferré, *Language*, p. 146.

63. *Ibid.*, pp. 148, 149.   64. *Ibid.*, pp. 160, 161.

65. *Ibid.*, pp. 163, 164.

66. Dorothy Emmet, *The Nature of Metaphysical Thinking* (London: Macmillan, 1945), p. 4.

67. *Op. cit.*, Ferré, *Language*, 195.

68. P. M. van Buren, *The Secular Meaning of the Gospel* (N.Y.: Macmillan, 1969), p. 103.

69. *Ibid.*, p. 84.   70. *Ibid.*, pp. 97, 99.

71. *Ibid.*, p. 102.   72. *Ibid.*, p. 134.   73. *Ibid.*, p. 156.

74. P. M. van Buren, *The Edges of Language* (N.Y.: Macmillan, 1972), p. 69.

75. *Ibid.*, p. 112.   76. *Ibid.*, pp. 144–145.

77. S. C. M. Press, London, 1963.

78. D. D. Evans, *The Logic of Self-Involvement* (London: S. C. M. Press, 1963), p. 39n.

79. D. D. Evans, "Differences Between Scientific and Religious Assertions," in *Science and Religion*, I. G. Barbour, ed. (N.Y.: Harper & Row, 1968), p. 112.

80. *Op. cit.*, *The Logic*, p. 108f.   81. *Ibid.*, p. 125.

82. *Ibid.*, p. 134.   83. *Ibid.*, p. 140.

84. D. M. High, *Language, Persons and Belief* (N.Y.: Oxford Univ. Press, 1967), p. iii.

85. *Ibid.*, pp. 67, 69.

86. Ludwig Wittgenstein, *Philosophical Investigations*, G. E. M. Anscombe, trans. (N.Y.: Macmillan, 1958), para. 19, p. 8e.

87. *Ibid.*, p. 226e.   88. *Op. cit.*, High, *Language*, p. 101.

89. *Ibid.*, p. 160.

90. See Ramsey's articles, "The Systematic Elusiveness of I," "Biology and Personality," "Human Personality," and "A Personal God."

91. *Op. cit.*, High, *Language*, p. 181.

CHAPTER IV

1. I am indebted to David L. Edwards for his insightful biography—*A Memoir* (London, Oxford University Press, 1973); Jerry H. Gill for his book on Ramsey in the "Contemporary Religious Thinkers Series," *Ian Ramsey: To Speak Responsibly of God* (London, Allen and Unwin, 1976); Donald Evans for his long article in *Religious Studies*, "Ian Ramsey on Talk About God" (*Religious Studies*, Vol. 7, Nos. 2 & 3, 6 & 9/1971); James W. McClendon, Jr., and James M. Smith for their article in the *Journal of the American Academy of Religion*, "Ian Ramsey's Model of Religious Language: A Qualified Appreciation" (*Journal of the American Academy of Religion*, Vol. 41, No. 3, 9/1973); which they later enlarged and used in their book *Understanding Religious Convictions* (Notre Dame, Indiana, University of Notre Dame Press, 1975); Terrence W. Tilley, for his analysis of Ramsey's contribution in *Talking of God* (New York, Paulist Press, 1978), and his article in the *JAAR Supplement*, "Ian Ramsey and Empirical Fit" (*Journal of the American Academy of Religion*, Vol. 45, No. 3, 9/1977); as well as the critical and sympathetic articles and reviews of H. D. Lewis, Ninian Smart, Cynthia B. Cohen, F. Michael McLain, R. B. Braithwaite, et. al., and others named elsewhere in this volume.

2. David L. Edwards, *Ian Ramsey: Bishop of Durham—A Memoir*, London, Oxford University Press, 1973, p. 23.

3. Ian Ramsey, "Contemporary Empiricism," in Jerry H. Gill, *Christian Empiricism*, London, Sheldon Press, 1974, p. 12.

4. Ian Ramsey, ed., *Locke: The Reasonableness of Christianity*, London, A. and C. Black, 1958, p. 20.

5. Ian Ramsey, *Religious Language*, London, S C M Press, 1957, p. 15.

6. Ian Ramsey, *Christian Discourse*, London, Oxford University Press, 1965, p. 1.

7. Edwards, *op. cit.*, p. 27.

8. Ian Ramsey, *Freedom and Immortality*, London, S C M Press, 1960, p. 152.

9. Ian Ramsey, ed., *Words About God*, London, S C M Press, 1971, p. 3.

10. Ian Ramsey, "On Understanding Mystery," in *Christian Empiricism*, p. 59.

11. Ian Ramsey, "Religion and Science: A Philosopher's Approach," in *Christian Empiricism*, p. 157.

12. Donald Evans, "Ian Ramsey on Talk About God," *Religious Studies*, Vol. 7, nos. 2 and 3 (June and September, 1971), p. 127.

13. *Ibid.*, pp. 127–128.   14.   *Ibid.*, p. 128.

15. Ramsey, *Religious Language*, p. 38.

16. Ian Ramsey, "The Systematic Elusiveness of 'I'," in *Christian Empiricism*, p. 17.

17. Ian Ramsey, ed., *Prospect for Metaphysics*, London, Allen and Unwin, 1961, p. 166.

18. Ian Ramsey, "Tubigen Lecture," in Edwards, *Ian Ramsey*, p. 34.

19. Ramsey, "The Systematic Elusiveness of 'I,' " pp. 23, 26.

20. Ian Ramsey, *Religion and Science*, London, S P C K, 1964.

21. Ian Ramsey, "Human Personality," in I. T. Ramsey and Ruth Porter, eds., *Personality and Science*, London, Churchill Livingstone, 1971, pp. 127–128.

22. Ramsey, *Prospect for Metaphysics*, p. 167.

23. Ramsey, "Human Personality," pp. 128–129.

24. Ramsey, *Christian Discourse*, p. 88.

25. Ian Ramsey, ed., *Christian Ethics and Contemporary Philosophy*, London, S C M Press, 1966, p. 169.

26. Ramsey, *Religious Language*, p. 72.

27. Ian Ramsey, "Reply," R. B. Braithwaite, et. al., "A Review: Models and Mystery," *Theoria to Theory*, Vol. 1 (3rd Quarter), (April, 1967), p. 266.

28. Ian Ramsey, *Models and Mystery*, London, Oxford University Press, 1964, p. 19.

29. Ramsey, "Reply," p. 268.

30. Cf., Ramsey, *Religious Language*, pp. 69–70.

31. *Ibid.*, pp. 23–24.   32. *Ibid.*, p. 15.

33. Ian Ramsey, "Religion and Science," p. 154.

34. Ramsey, *Religious Language*, pp. 23–24.

35. Cf., *Ibid.*, pp. 28–35 and 42–47, etc.

36. Ramsey, *Models and Mystery*, p. 58.

37. Ramsey, *Religious Language*, p. 36.   38. *Ibid.*, p. 18.

39. Ramsey, *Models and Mystery*, p. 44.

40. Ramsey, *Religious Language*, p. 47.

41. Ian Ramsey, Mimeographed Lecture Notes for "Philosophy of Religion."

42. Ian Ramsey, "The Logical Character of Resurrection Belief," in *Christian Empiricism*, p. 179.

43. Ramsey, *Religious Language*, p. 37.

44. Ian Ramsey, "A Personal God," in *Prospect for Theology*, F. G. Healey, ed., London, Nisbet, 1966, p. 69.

45. Ramsey, *Prospect for Metaphysics*, p. 176.

46. Ramsey, "Paradox in Religion" in *Christian Empiricism*, p. 111.

47. Donald Evans, "Ian Ramsey on Talk About God," p. 138.

48. Ian Ramsey, "Moral Judgments and God's Commands," in *Christian Ethics and Contemporary Philosophy*, London, S C M Press, 1966, p. 152.

49. Ramsey, *Models and Mystery*, p. 59.   50. *Ibid.*, p. 60.

51. Ramsey, *Religious Language*, p. 61.

52. Ithaca, N.Y., Cornell University Press, 1962.

53. Ved Mehata, *The New Theologian*, N.Y., Harper & Row, 1965, p. 119.

54. Ramsey, *Models and Mystery*, p. 50.   55. *Ibid.*, p. 56.

56. Ramsey, *Religious Language*, p. 62.

57. *Ibid.*, p. 69.   58. *Ibid.*, p. 53.

59. Ian Ramsey, "On Understanding Mystery," in *Christian Empiricism*, pp. 71–72.

60. *Ibid.*, p. 70.   61. *Ibid.*, pp. 70–71.   62. *Ibid.*, p. 72.

63. Ian Ramsey, *On Being Sure in Religion*, London, The Athlone Press, 1963, pp. 17–18.

64. Ramsey, *Religious Language*, pp. 79–80.

65. *Ibid.*, pp. 84–85.   66. *Ibid.*, p. 106.   67. *Ibid.*, p. 111.

68. Ian Ramsey, "On Being Articulate About the Gospel," in *Christian Empiricism*, pp. 76–77.

69. *Ibid.*, p. 77.   70. Ramsey, *Religious Language*, p. 170.

71. *Ibid.*, pp. 173–174.   72. *Ibid.*, p. 179.

73. Ian Ramsey, ed., *Words About God*, London, S C M Press, 1971, p. 17.

74. "A Logical Exploration of Some Christian Doctrines," *Chicago Theological Seminary Register*, Vol. LIII, No. 5 (May, 1963), p. 38.

75. Ramsey, *Models and Mystery*, p. 67.

76. G. J. Warnock, *English Philosophy Since 1900*, London, Oxford University Press, 1958, p. 144.

77. Ramsey, *Religious Language*, p. 10.

78. Ramsey, *Prospect for Metaphysics*, pp. 162–163.

79. Ramsey, *Religion and Science,* pp. 42–43.

80. Ramsey, *Prospect for Metaphysics,* pp. 173–174.

81. *Ibid.,* p. 176.   82. *Ibid.,* p. 161.

83. Ramsey, *Religion and Science,* p. 76.

84. *Ibid.,* p. 80.   85. Ramsey, *On Being Sure in Religion,* p. 3.

86. *Ibid.,* p. 27.   87. Ramsey, *Religious Language,* p. 186.

88. Ramsey, *Models and Mystery,* p. 19.

89. Ramsey, *Religious Language,* p. 48.

90. Ramsey, "Religion and Science, A Philosopher's Approach," pp. 17 and 52.

91. Ramsey, *Words About God,* pp. 214–215.

92. Ramsey, *Models and Mystery,* p. 17.

93. Ramsey, "Models and Mystery: Reply," p. 267.

94. Ian Ramsey, *Models for Divine Activity,* London, S C M Press, 1973, p. 64.

95. T. W. Tilley, "Ian Ramsey and Empirical Fit," *Journal of the American Academy of Religion,* Vol. 45, No. 3, Supplement (September, 1977), p. 982.

CHAPTER V

1. *Hibbert Journal,* LIV (4/1956), pp. 242ff.   2. *Ibid.,* p. 250.

3. *Hibbert Journal,* LIV (6/1956), pp. 330ff.

4. *Ibid.,* p. 334.   5. *Ibid.,* p. 338.

6. *Cambridge Review* (3/3/56), pp. 404–5 and (3/10/56), pp. 433–6. Reprinted in *Christian Ethics and Contemporary Philosophy,* Ian Ramsey, ed. London, S. C. M. Press, 1966, pp. 53–73; pp. 84–94.

7. *Ibid.,* pp. 85–6.   8. *Ibid.,* p. 94.

9. N.Y. Abingdon Press, 1958.   10. *Ibid.,* p. 68.

11. *Hibbert Journal,* LIX (1/1961); reprinted in *Christian Empiricism,* J. H. Gill, ed. London, Sheldon Press, 1974, pp. 207ff.

12. "Some Further Reflections on Freedom and Immortality," *Hibbert Journal,* LIX (7/1961); also reprinted in *Christian Empiricism,* pp. 219ff.

13. Lewis, *op. cit.,* p. 211.   14. Ramsey, *op. cit.,* p. 228.

15. *Ibid.,* p. 228.   16. London, Eyre & Spottiswoode, 1962.

17. *Ibid.,* p. 141.

18. *Proceedings of the Aristotelian Society,* Supplementary Volume 33 (1959), pp. 219ff. Reprinted in *Christian Empiricism,* op. cit., pp. 98ff.

19. *Theology,* LXVIII, No. 535 (1/1965), pp. 31ff. Reprinted in *Christian Empiricism, op. cit.,* pp. 229ff.

20. *Ibid.*, pp. 229–30.   21. *Ibid.*, pp. 231–32.

22. *Theology*, LXVIII, No. 536 (2/1965), pp. 109ff. Reprinted in *Christian Empiricism, op. cit.*, pp. 237ff.

23. *Ibid.*, p. 239.

24. "Talking About God: Models, Ancient and Modern," *Myth and Symbol*, F. W. Dillistone, ed. London, S. P. C. K., 1966.

25. London, Oxford University Press, 1965.

26. "Christian Education *Post Mortem Dei*," *Religious Education*, LX, No. 1, (102/1965).

27. *Theoria to Theory*, Vol. 1, (4/1967), pp. 250ff.

28. Ian Ramsey, *Religious Language*, London, S. C. M. Press, 1957, p. 47.

29. *Theoria to Theory, op. cit.*, p. 255.   30. *Ibid.*, p. 257.

31. Ian Ramsey, *Models and Mystery*, London, Oxford University Press, 1964, p. 58.

32. *Theoria to Theory, op. cit.*, p. 262.

33. N.Y., Harper & Row, 1967.

34. Ian Ramsey, *Models and Mystery, op. cit.*, p. 44.

35. Macquarrie, *God-Talk, op. cit.*, p. 232.   36. *Ibid.*, p. 232.

37. Indianapolis, Bobbs Merrill, 1969.

38. Gilkey, *Naming the Whirlwind, op. cit.*, pp. 235, 287.

39. *Journal of the American Academy of Religion*, Vol. 38, No. 3 (9/1970) pp. 240ff.

40. *Ibid.*, p. 246.   41. *Ibid.*, p. 251.

42. *Religious Studies*, Vol. 7, Nos. 2 & 3, (6/1971), pp. 125ff and 213ff.

43. *Ibid.*, No. 3, pp. 225–226.

44. *Theology*, Vol. 74, No. 608 (2/1971), pp. 67ff.

45. *Ibid.*, pp. 69–70.   46. Boston, Allyn and Bacon, 1971.

47. *Ibid.*, p. 29.

48. *International Journal for Philosophy of Religion*, Vol. 3, No. 1, (Spring, 1972), pp. 2ff.

49. *Religious Studies*, Vol. 9, No. 2 (6/1973), pp. 143ff.

50. C. B. Cohen, "Some Aspects of Ian Ramsey's Empiricism," *op. cit.*, p. 17.

51. C. B. Cohen, "The Logic of Religious Language," *op. cit.*, p. 150.

52. *Ibid.*, p. 155.

53. London, Cambridge University Press, 1973.

54. Ian Ramsey, *Religious Language, op. cit.*, p. 131.

55. Roger Trigg, *Reason and Commitment, op. cit.*, p. 79.

56. *Journal of the American Academy of Religion*, Vol. 41, No. 3, (9/1973) pp. 413ff.

57. Notre Dame, University of Notre Dame Press, 1975.

58. McClendon and Smith, "Ian Ramsey's Model of Religious Language," *op. cit.*, p. 417.

59. *Ibid.*, p. 421.   60. New York, Hawthorn Books, 1976.

61. *Ibid.*, p. 34.   62. *Ibid.*, p. 35.

63. *Journal of the American Academy of Religion*, Vol. 45, No. 3, Supplement (9/1977), pp. 964ff.

64. New York, Paulist Press, 1978.

65. *Prospect for Theology*, F. G. Healey, ed., London, Nisbet, 1967.

66. Tilley, *op. cit.*, p. 91.

67. *Teachers' College Record*, Vol. 68, No. 7 (4/1967).

68. *The Journal of Religious Thought*, Vol. 27, No. 1 (Spring-Summer/ 1970).

69. Ian Ramsey, Oxford Lecture Notes, undated.

70. Reprinted in *Christian Empiricism*, J. H. Gill, ed. London, Sheldon Press, 1974, p. 16.

71. Ramsey, *Models and Mystery*, p. 60.

Selected Bibliography

Principal Works of Ian T. Ramsey

"Miracles: An Exercise in Logical Mapwork" (Oxford Inaugural Lecture), Oxford, Clarendon Press, 1952.

"The Challenge of Contemporary Philosophy to Christianity," *Modern Churchman*, Vol. 42, 1952.

"Christianity and Language," *Philosophical Quarterly*, Vol. 4, 1954.

"The Systematic Elusiveness of 'I'," *Philosophical Quarterly*, Vol. 5, No. 20, 7/1955.

"The Paradox of Omnipotence," *Mind*, Vol. 65, No. 258, 4/1956.

"Empiricism and Religion," *The Christian Scholar*, Vol. 39, No. 2, 6/1956.

"Persons and Funerals: What Do Person Words Mean?," *Hibbert Journal*, Vol. 54, 6/1956.

"Religion and Empiricism: III," *Cambridge Review*, Vol. 77, 1956.

"The Logical Character of Resurrection-belief," *Theology*, Vol. 60, No. 443, 5/1957.

"Ethics and Reason," *Church Quarterly Review*, Vol. 158, Spring, 1957.

Religious Language, London, S. C. M. Press, 1957.

John Locke, *The Reasonableness of Christianity* (editor), London, Adam & Charles Black, 1958.

"Paradox in Religion," *Proceedings of the Aristotelian Society*, Supplementary Vol. 33, 1959.

"Contemporary Empiricism," *The Christian Scholar*, Vol. 43, No. 3, Fall, 1960.

Freedom and Immortality, London, S. C. M. Press, 1960.

"Religion and Science: A Philosopher's Approach," *Church Quarterly Review*, Vol. 157, Winter, 1961.

"Some Further Reflections on *Freedom and Immortality*," *Hibbert Journal*, 59, 7/1961.

"The Challenge of the Philosophy of Language," *London Quarterly and Holborn Review*, Vol. 186, 1961.

Prospect for Metaphysics (editor), London, Allen & Unwin, 1961.

"On Understanding Mystery," "Theological Literacy," "On Being Articulate About the Gospel," and "A Logical Exploration of Some Christian Doctrines," *Chicago Theological Seminary Register*, Vol. 53, No. 5, 5/1963.

On Being Sure in Religion, London, Athlone Press, 1963.

"Towards the Relevant in Theological Language," *Modern Churchman*, Vol. 8, 10/1964.

"History and the Gospels: Some Philosophical Reflections," *Studia Evangelica: III* (Berlin), Vol. 88, 1964.

"Biology and Personality," *Philosophical Forum*, Vol. 21, 1964.

Models and Mystery, London, Oxford University Press, 1964.

Religion and Science: Conflict and Synthesis, London, S. P. C. K., 1964.

"Letter to the Editor," *Theology*, Vol. 68, No. 536, 2/1965.

"The Authority of the Church Today," *Authority and the Church*, R. R. Williams, ed., London, S. P. C. K., 1965.

Christian Discourse: Some Logical Explorations, London, Oxford University Press, 1965.

Biology and Personality (editor), Oxford, Blackwell, 1965.

"Talking About God: Models Ancient and Modern," *Myth and Symbol*, F. W. Dillistone, editor, London, S. P. C. K., 1966.

Christian Ethics and Contemporary Philosophy (editor), London, S. C. M. Press, 1966.

"A Personal God," *Prospect for Theology*, F. G. Healy, editor, Welwyn, Herts, Nisbet, 1966.

"Models and Mystery," Discussion: Braithwaite, Miller, Bastian; reply by Ramsey, *Theoria to Theory*, Vol. 1, 1967.

"Polanyi and J. L. Austin," *Intellect and Hope*, T. Langford and W. H. Poteat, editors, Durham, Duke University Press, 1968.

"The Concept of the Eternal," *The Christian Hope*, London, S. P. C. K., 1970.

Our Understanding of Prayer, London, S. P. C. K., 1971.

Words About God, London, S. C. M. Press, 1971.

Personality and Science, Ramsey and Ruth Porter, editors, London, Churchill Livingstone, 1971.

Models for Divine Activity, London, S. C. M. Press, 1973.

Christian Empiricism, J. H. Gill, editor, London, Sheldon Press, 1974.

Books About Ian T. Ramsey

Edwards, David L., *Ian Ramsey, Bishop of Durham: A Memoir*, London, Oxford University Press, 1973.

Gill, Jerry H., *Ian Ramsey: To Speak Responsibly of God*, London, Allen & Unwin, 1974.